Imagining Redemption

IMAGINING REDEMPTION

David H. Kelsey

WJK WESTMINSTER
JOHN KNOX PRESS
LOUISVILLE • KENTUCKY

Book design by Sharon Adams
Cover design by Mark Abrams

First edition
Published by Westminster John Knox Press
Louisville, Kentucky

This book is printed on acid-free paper that meets the American National Standards Institute Z39.48 standard. ⊗

PRINTED IN THE UNITED STATES OF AMERICA

05 06 07 08 09 10 11 12 13 14 — 10 9 8 7 6 5 4 3 2 1

Library of Congress Cataloging-in-Publication Data is on file at the Library of Congress, Washington, D.C.

ISBN 0-664-22889-5

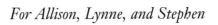

For Allison, Lynne, and Stephen

Contents

Contents

Acknowledgments

This book is an expansion of the Taylor Lectures that I delivered at Yale Divinity School's annual convocation in 2004. I wish to express my gratitude to my colleagues on the Divinity School faculty for the honor of the invitation to be the Taylor lecturer, and to Dean and Mrs. Harry Attridge for the school's generous hospitality during convocation week.

The book draws on a variety of experiences over an extended period of time during which I have incurred debts to more people than I can name. It had its genesis almost twenty years ago on a long walk on the Block Island, Rhode Island, beach, during which my wife Julie and I talked about the story of Sam's family, recounted here, and she suggested that it could be an excellent occasion for theological reflection on suffering, evil, and redemption. We have come back to the subject repeatedly; without her gentle insistence that it was an important project, this book would never have materialized. Invitations to deliver a Lenten Series at Trinity Episcopal Church, Southport, Connecticut, and a course in the Lay School of Theology at St. Luke's Episcopal Church, Darien, Connecticut, gave me opportunities to try out different approaches to the topic. I am grateful to the people and clergy of those congregations for the readiness with which they engaged, challenged, and encouraged me in what I had to say. I am also in the debt of Yale Divinity School students in the seminar "Evil and the Kingdom of God," which I taught alternate years for over a decade, and most especially to my late colleague Professor Leon Watts, with whom I team-taught the seminar the last two times it was offered. Along with works of academic theology, we read autobiography and fiction, slave narratives, and William Styron's *Sophie's Choice*. From Professor Watts I learned how narratives of evil undergone can themselves be theological documents about redemption. Several people very generously read in manuscript either the lectures or the book and offered astute critique and advice, especially Julie Kelsey, Allison Claire, Lynne Kelsey, and Barbara Wheeler. I have been saved by them from some serious mistakes and infelicities, even though I have not always followed their guidance. Remaining errors and awkwardness, of course, are my fault. No one has worked more closely with the manuscript than Stephanie Egnotovich, my editor at Westminster John Knox Press, and I am profoundly grateful to her for shepherding this book to publication and for her enthusiastic, detailed, thorough, and tactful care in making it as readable as it is.

9 June 2004
Colomba of Iona

Imagining Redemption

1

What Earthly Difference Can Jesus Make Here?

Milton was the first colleague I met the fall I began teaching in an undergraduate Religion Department. He had just been appointed the college organist. On Sundays Milt also served as organist-choirmaster at the local Episcopal parish. It turned out that we had several mutual acquaintances at our respective graduate schools, our wives had similar interests, and we had young children roughly the same age. As junior faculty tend to do, the four of us began to hang out together.

The following spring on the first warm sunny Sunday afternoon, our two families took off with kids, strollers, charcoal grills, and coolers to a nearby state park for a picnic. As we settled into our first drink Milt said, "Well, I think I caused a real flap in church this morning."

I immediately assumed that the choir must have royally messed up and Milt's artistic temperament had got the better of his churchly decorum. Not at all. The stir had happened at the adult education forum between the two morning services. Someone made a presentation about the *Book of Common Prayer* and an opportunity for questions followed. But nobody said a thing.

"So I got to my feet and I said, 'We hear all the time in church about redemption. We hear that word in sermons, in the Scripture readings, and it's all over the liturgy. Will somebody please tell me what that word means?'"

"What did they say?" the novice theologian asked, all ready to offer doctrinal amendments, corrections, and complexifications.

"Nobody said anything."

For a few seconds this seemed funny. Then I was appalled. I didn't know whether to laugh or to groan.

This conversation has haunted me. How should redemption be thought about and imagined? That is the question I want to explore in this book. What do people in communities of Christian faith mean when they affirm that redemption happens or pray for it to happen? What should they take it to mean for their own lives when they read their Scriptures' witnesses to redemptive events?

WHERE WE'RE TALKING FROM

There is, I believe, no one answer to Milton's question. There are three reasons for this, and all of them share the context out of which both the question about redemption and this discussion come.

First, the question about redemption usually arises with personal urgency when it concerns some particular, concrete situation or event. I argue in this book that what "redemption" concretely means for Christians is relative to the concrete particularities of the situations and events that cry out for redemption. There can therefore be no one meaning of redemption that covers all cases.

Second, Milton's question about redemption came out of a context defined by the common life of a Christian congregation in which the term *redemption* and its related terms are used in a multitude of ways. There are rules that, at least implicitly, govern those uses of *redemption*, and coherent remarks that can be made about those uses; but no one use can be identified as being the core or primary "theological meaning" of this family of words.

Third, the question about redemption was asked by a person shaped by his context in twentieth-century American culture. In that culture, *redemption* and related terms are used in colloquial English in a variety of ways that, I suggest, are extended metaphorically in Christian talk about God's redeeming.

These three points together, I shall argue, mean that while there are many ways to answer Milton's question properly, there is no one basic or proper meaning of "redemption," Christianly speaking.

Guided by the first point, the centrality of concrete situation, I will focus in chapters 2 through 4 on a sequence of terrible events and situations experienced by a single family and ask what could count as redemption from that set of events and situations. Guided by the second point, the various meanings of Christian redemption, I will explore in each chapter Christian accounts of who Jesus is and how God relates redemptively in and through him and what these suggest about the meaning of redemption in this concrete situation. Guided by the third point, our cultural context, each chapter explores one way in which an everyday English meaning of the word *redemption* can be extended metaphorically in Christian talk about God's relating redemptively in Jesus Christ to this one concrete situation.

Before we begin, however, we must be clear about our starting point, for this discussion cannot be conducted, as it were, from nowhere. Our exploration of meanings of *redemption* originates at the intersection of two contexts.

Milton asked his question in the midst of the common life of one Christian congregation and about practices that are central to the common life of all communities of Christian faith—practices of preaching; practices of living with Scripture in study, prayer, and liturgy; and practices of worship of God. As Milton observed about these practices, the word *redemption* is "all over them." Since I want to explore answers to Milt's question here, the context of my exploration will be communities of Christian faith and practice. I will explore ways in which "that word" may be understood *Christianly*.

Thinking and talking about redemption, or about anything else for that matter, is always thought and talk *from* somewhere, from some particular context. Acknowledgment of this fact is partially captured by the cliché that what you think and say "all depends on your point of view." The cliché, however, distorts the insight it seeks to express.

The distortion comes into focus if we reflect on the contrast between a "point" and a "context." A point is an abstraction, lacking all dimensions. There is no "there" there. No human person can live on a point. No one can really occupy some one "point" for viewing the world. The phrase "point of view" suggests a clearly formulated, coherent intellectual position, perhaps based on a few basic governing principles, with which one can embrace, organize, and interpret all of experience. It is, of necessity, abstracted from the messiness, contingency, and oddity of everyday life. Whatever may be the case with certain systematic bodies of theory about the world, there cannot be a "Christian point of view" because there is no "Christian point" abstracted from the messy particularities of life from which to have such a view.

We do live, however, in contexts, and sometimes we want to describe a given context in which we live to someone who doesn't share it. That poses a challenge. We sense that our context has a number of dimensions, and we have acquired a rhetoric in which to describe each of them. So we have one rhetoric for describing its physical dimension, such as its terrain or its climate, and quite another for describing its psychological dimension, say its emotional dynamics or the dominant feelings we have living in it. We have yet another rhetoric for describing our context's social dimension, say its class structure, which isn't quite the same as the rhetoric we use to describe its cultural dimension, say its racial or ethnic makeup. Most of these rhetorics are derived from and presuppose some body of appropriate theory, whether geological, climatological, psychological, sociological, cultural, anthropological, and so on. The challenge is that these various rhetorics are often quite abstract so that when we've finished trying to describe the context in which we live, with all its multiple dimensions, we feel frustrated that somehow its concrete particularity has slipped through the verbal net we've been weaving and our listener has gathered only a thin and vague sense of just where concretely we actually live.

This frustration has been especially challenging for cultural anthropologists whose professional work turns on describing for their readers the often very alien social and cultural contexts of the communities they have studied in their field research. To meet this challenge, some of them have undertaken to give what anthropologist Clifford Geertz calls "thick descriptions" of the societies and cultures that they study. A thick description attempts to give a holistic description of the multidimensional social and cultural context of a community's life that conveys it in its concrete particularity. It does so not by analyzing that context according to some body of theory or combination of theories, but by giving carefully detailed, anecdotal accounts, almost like short stories, of interactions that take place as members of the community being studied engage in practices that make up their common life across a significant period of time.

As they enact those practices, members of those communities move about in their multidimensional contextual space—"move about" not just physically but also socially, psychologically, culturally, sometimes politically, sometimes economically, sometimes religiously. Those practices are at once linguistic and bodily practices. As linguistic practices they are characteristic ways of speaking to one another about what they are doing while they are doing it, ways of speaking that often also "locate" them in relation to one another socially, culturally, psychologically, economically, politically, and so on. As bodily interactions they have characteristic patterns that are learned in just that context and are also expressive of persons' "locations" in relation to those with whom they interact. The point is that it is those practices that concretely constitute the location in which and from which members of a community think and speak. The practices concretely make up the context in which the community lives.

Accordingly, what members of communities of Christian faith say about God, the world, and themselves is said not from some comprehensive, systematic Christian "point of view," but from the context in which they live. It is said out of an array of practices that make up both the common life of communities of Christian faith and the individual lives of their members. Hence what Christians say in particular about redemption of experienced evil comes out of a context of living, a social and linguistic space constituted by the practices that make up Christians' common life. It is a capacious social space that embraces a variety of ways of living faithfully. And it is a flexible linguistic space that makes possible vigorous and deep disagreement and debate about such matters as, for example, the nature of humankind's need for redemption and the character of God's redemptive relating to the human scene. I address Milton's question out of that context.

The social and linguistic space constituted by the set of practices that make up the common life of communities of Christian faith intersects with another context: that is, the social and linguistic space constituted by practices that make up the common life of the larger societies and cultures within which communities of Christian faith are located. Members of Christian communities inescapably live in both contexts. In the case of both Milton's question and my effort to address his question, the relevant contexts of communities of Christian faith are North American societies and cultures.

The language of redemption is used in a variety of ways in this larger social and cultural context. For example, as an assiduous reader of reviews of fiction, plays, and movies, I have been impressed by the frequency with which reviewers comment on the presence or absence of a "redemptive" note or theme in the work under review or debate whether there might be such a note. Sometimes the presence of a redemptive note seems to count in favor of the work and its absence to count against it. Although I am often unable to tell just what the reviewer means by "redemption" or "redemptive," it is clear that the words are used in the context of certain practices that help make up Western cultural life. At least some of the time the supposition seems to be that these words name one possible basis by which to critique enactments of these practices (for example, the practices that constitute writing a novel, performing a play, or making a movie).

Members of communities of Christian faith and practice thus also participate in the practices that make up the cultural life of the societies that are their immediate social and cultural contexts and routinely use "redeem," "redemption," and related terms in ways that are not peculiarly Christian as well as in ways that are. Furthermore, their extra-Christian uses of these terms doubtless shape the way they use them in the context of the common life of Christian faith communities, and vice versa. I address Milton's question out of this context as well.

The distinction between how the word "redeem" is used in the common life of communities of Christian faith and how it is used in the larger cultures in which those communities are set requires us to identify some distinguishing features of Christian uses of the word.

SPEAKING OF REDEMPTION CHRISTIANLY

Before anything else, I must reformulate Milton's question about redemption to read: *What earthly difference can Jesus make here?*

The reasons for reformulating the question this way lie in the various ways that Christians typically speak of redemption. At least five features of such talk restrict not only the way we answer Milton's question but also the way we ask it. While we will return to each of them in more detail in the next three chapters, it will be helpful if I outline them here. As I shall show, these features of typically Christian talk of redemption require my reformulation of Milt's question.

What follows are brief generalizations about Christian redemption-talk across the centuries. I do not doubt that significant exceptions can be found to each of these generalizations. All the same, they seem on balance to be roughly correct.

1. First, Christians tend to speak of redemption in terms of *an act of relating that makes a difference to the person or situation being related to.* The expressions "to redeem" and "redemption" qualify a particular relationship as "redemptive," that is, as making a redemptive difference. This redemptive relationship is active. It is not just a static given, somehow just "there." It is not, for example, analogous to the structural fact that all mammals depend on their environment for air and food and that their environment, in turn, is altered by their consuming part of it and breathing out into it. Nor is it analogous to the relation of dependency that helpless human infants have with their parents. Such relations might be thought of as structural relations that are built into and essential to being human, necessarily exhibited by every human being at some or every stage of its life. Any entity that does not exhibit such structural relations would not be a human being.

Nor is the relation called "redemption" analogous to those relations that human beings create by actively relating to one another—say, in friendship, or in animosity, or as a business or marriage partner, as fellow citizen or outlaw. The abstract possibility of relating to other human beings in these ways is inherent in being human, a structural feature of human being. Any entity that does not exhibit such structural relations is not a human being.

In contrast, the relation Christians call "being redeemed" is created by an agent other than the human beings who are in need of redemption—an agent who can be named, actively relating to the human scene. The agent doing this active relating solely determines that the relation exists between the human scene and that agent. This is part of what Christians have meant by characterizing redemption as "grace." The relation is not a built-in structural feature of being human, and if there were no such relating, human beings would still be human creatures.

The very character of the relation Christians call "redemption" also depends on the character of the one who actively relates redemptively. If some other agent, having a different nature, were to relate to whatever in the human scene requires redemption, or if the relation were in fact a structure universally built into human being and essential to it, or if it were a relation human beings could create for themselves, then it would not be the relation Christians call "redemption"; it would be some other relation.

This emphasis on the active nature of "redeeming" highlights the following crucial point: being redeemed is a relation that makes some kind of difference to those who are being related to. "Redemption" names just that difference. My effort to explain what "redemption" means is an effort to explain what that difference is.

Accordingly, the question about the meaning of *redemption*, Christianly speaking, must be reframed as a question that begins "What *difference*. . . ," with the understanding that the difference is a "redemptive" difference, whatever that may turn out to mean.

But this does not yet say what *redemption* itself means. It only tells us that if talk of redemption is going to count as typically Christian talk, then it must be framed in the following way: *Whatever* "redemption" means, it is an active relating that makes a difference to the persons or situations being related to. So we reframe the question to ask, "What *difference* does 'redemption' make?"

2. That point leads immediately into a second feature of typical Christian talk about redemption. The active relating that Christians call "redemption" is complex, and its complexity lies in just who is doing the redemptive relating.

On the one hand, Christians tend to speak of God as the one who relates to the human scene redemptively. That is, they use the phrase "to redeem" to name one way in which God relates to the human scene. This way God relates is different from and in addition to how, for example, God relates to create, relates to rule, or relates to draw to eschatological consummation. In Christian uses of "redeem," God is the active subject and redemption qualifies the action. Indeed, it is God alone who can relate to creation redemptively.

On the other hand, this is far too simple a description, for Christians characteristically say Jesus Christ is the subject who actively relates redemptively to the human scene. They use the word "redemption" in relation to Christ, and by definition, that is what makes their talk about redemption specifically "Christian" talk.

What makes the redemptive relation of which Christians speak so complex is the way they understand the relation between God and Jesus. According to the Gospels' narratives, the God who redeems does so by relating to Jesus in a special way, thereby relating to us in a special way; and the Jesus who redeems does so by relating back to God in a special way while relating to us in a special way.

The Gospel narratives of what Jesus did and underwent describe who Jesus is, his unsubstitutable personal identity. As they tell it, *in* what he did and underwent Jesus related to his fellow human beings as one who was, wholly and without reservation, *for* them, for their liberation from powers that bound them. He shared their common lot in complete solidarity with them in their suffering and oppression. They also tell of Jesus' responding in the power of the Holy Spirit to the One he called "Father," relating to God in unqualified self-giving trust.

At the same time, the Gospels weave in and throughout the narratives of what Jesus does and undergoes another narrative, a story of God working to redeem the human scene. In these stories Jesus' relating to us is *itself* God relating redemptively to us.

Thus, Christians characteristically talk about redemption in a God-centered or theocentric way; whatever "redemption" means, only God can relate to the human scene "redemptively." They do not speak, however, of redemption in a generically theistic way; the God who relates redemptively is not God-in-general, "the great divine whatever." Rather, in Christian talk, the God who relates redemptively is explicitly understood *in terms of the story of Jesus.* The story of that person is definitive of who God is. Whatever "redemption" means, Jesus defines the God who does it. The redeemer is defined by God's relation to Jesus and Jesus' relation to God in the power of the Spirit. The complexity of their relationship defines *who* it is that relates to humankind to redeem. Not only is redemption understood in a Christ-centered way, which might suggest that Jesus Christ is merely the instrument God uses to relate redemptively to human beings, but the *agent* (God) who relates redemptively is also defined christocentrically. Just that and only that complex relationship among God, Jesus, the Holy Spirit, and us humans is what Christians typically have in mind when they talk of God relating to us redemptively.

Accordingly, our attempt to understand redemption has to be an attempt to understand not what we might call God-in-general-redeeming, but rather more particularly what redemptive difference *Jesus*—this one concrete person in his unsubstitutable personal identity—could make.

But this does not yet say or imply what *redemption* itself means. It only tells us that if talk about God relating redemptively is going to count as typically Christian talk about redemption it must be framed christocentrically. To imagine redemption of any concrete situation is to interpret it as included within Jesus' story. So we reframe our question to ask, "What (redemptive) difference can *Jesus* make?"

3. Christians tend to assume that what God relates to redemptively are *concrete human beings in concrete circumstances* that are in need of redemption. The very idea of God relating to the human scene redemptively implies that there is something about the human scene that stands in need of redemption.

Is it the human-scene-as-such-and-as-a-whole that stands in need of redemption? The apostle Paul talks about how the human scene has fallen subject to the power of sin, the law, and death (Rom. 6–8); and how the world is in the grip of principalities (Rom. 8:38) and elemental spirits (Gal. 4:3, 9). Colossians and Ephesians speak of the world as subject to powers and principalities (Col. 2:15; Eph. 6:12 [KJV]). The Synoptic Gospels and John assume that our lived worlds are ruled and distorted by Satan and a population of evil spirits. The Apocalypse of John sees the world subject to the power of the Devil (2:10; 12:9; 20:2). To the extent that such New Testament writings are paradigmatic for Christian talk about redemption, it could easily seem that such talk assumes that what cries out for redemption is the world as such, the embracing creaturely context in which human beings live.

That is just what has sometimes been assumed in the history of Christian talk about redemption. When this assumption is made, talk of redemption tends to rely on a dualistic picture of the human scene, in which human beings are prisoners in an inherently evil world against which a good God fights to redeem them. Christian talk of redemption that assumes the validity of such a picture risks either (1) implicitly denying the goodness of the world God created or (2) denying the goodness of the one who created the world and affirming the view that the good God who redeems is different from the evil one who created. Most Christians, however, have wished to avoid running those risks in their talk about redemption.

More nuanced Christian accounts have characteristically not focused on the human scene in general as that which is in need of redemption. Instead, they have assumed that it is concrete human beings and their concrete particular circumstances that stand in need of redemption. This view follows paradigms provided by the New Testament. After all, when the apostle Paul talks about redemption, he is addressing the particular circumstances of particular people in particular churches. No doubt, he believes that the world is in the grip of evil powers and principalities, but that belief serves as background to what he says about the redemption of the concrete circumstances of particular people, and he invokes it only as the background to what he has to say about redemption. So too, while the Gospels may well assume that this world is dominated by evil spirits, when they narrate Jesus' earthly ministry they focus on his active relating to concrete particular people in concrete particular circumstances—his friend Simon's ill mother, Bartimaeus the blind roadside beggar, socially outcast lepers, a demon-possessed madman in chains, the synagogue leader Jairus in anguish over his young daughter's mortal illness, a pagan Roman Centurion distraught over his servant's deadly illness, Mary and Martha in despair that their brother Lazarus had died and Jesus had not gotten there to help. And the Apocalypse of John, while it certainly assumes that the human-scene-as-such is in need of redemption from its bondage to Satan, focuses on the particular community that is persecuted by the Roman Empire because of its faithful witness to Jesus.

It has been typical of Christian talk of redemption to follow these New Testament patterns and find concrete human beings in concrete circumstances to be that which stands in need of redemption. Accordingly, our question about the meaning of "redemption" Christianly speaking must be reframed as a question that asks, "What difference can Jesus make *here?*" that is, for some particular persons in some concrete situations.

But we have still not yet said what *redemption* itself means. The previous discussion only tells us that if talk of redemption is going to count as typically Christian talk it must be framed so that whatever "redemption" turns out to mean, it has to do with concrete particular circumstances and the persons involved in them. For that reason, in chapters 2 through 4 I will focus on the story of a sequence of situations that befell one particular family.

4. This last point needs to be sharpened in one important respect. Christian talk about redemption tends to be based on the assumption

that concrete particular people in particular circumstances *stand in need of redemption in two general situations:* (1) When they actively sin and are guilty; and (2) in situations of horrific evil that befall them. In the abstract these two situations can be distinguished reasonably clearly. One major difference between them is that the sin and guilt from which particular people need to be redeemed is something they actively do and incur in particular and concrete circumstances, while the evil that needs to be redeemed is something that befalls them in particular and concrete circumstances. Hence an important distinction between these two sorts of redemption involves the connection between redemption and human responsibility.

Christian talk about redemption in relation to sin is regularly accompanied by talk about human responsibility for the sin done, the guilt incurred by doing it, the resulting estrangement from God, God's judgment and forgiveness, and reconciliation with God despite the sin. Efforts to understand how God redeems sin are typically classified under the theological label "atonement" and focus on Jesus as the agent of at-one-ment. In the context of talk about atonement of sin, Christians typically associate the word "redemption" with reconciliation with God, forgiveness by God, justification of the sinner, sanctification of the sinner, and "salvation" of sinners in the sense of their extrication or rescue from the dire consequences of sin.

By contrast, Christian talk about redemption in relation to horrendous evils that befall people does not turn on human responsibility. Instead, it is regularly accompanied by talk about the suffering, distortion, and brokenness of life that evil inflicts on people; the re-creation of their lives and the worlds in which they live; the destruction of evil's power to distort and break creaturely life; and the consummation of those lives in a fulfillment blessed with a type of life otherwise unavailable to them. Efforts to understand how God redeems the evil that human beings undergo are typically classified under the theological label *eschatology*. While Jesus is certainly involved, eschatologically related discussion of redemption tends to focus on God's power over evil. In the context of talk about eschatological victory over the power of evil, Christians typically associate the word *redemption* with the promise of a new creation, the actualization of that promise beginning here and now, the inauguration in history of the "kingdom of God" and God's reign of justice and peace, the ultimate consummation of creatures in a participation in the very life of God, and "salvation" in the etymologically correct sense of "healing" or "making whole" creatures who have been broken by horrific evils.

Thus Christian talk about redemption suggests that, at least in the abstract, there are two different types of things from which human beings need to be redeemed: things they do and things that they undergo. For convenience' sake, we can designate one "redemption understood in terms of atonement" and the other "redemption understood in terms of eschatology." The first is redemption despite persons' own responsibility for what requires redemption; the second is redemption of that for which persons are not themselves responsible.

In the messiness of actual life, these two ways that human beings need redemption are usually thoroughly enmeshed with each other. As I noted previously, Christians have tended to suppose that Jesus can make a redemptive difference to a concrete person's particular sinful doing or particular suffering undergone, and that in their concrete particularity both tend to be inseparably entangled. Human beings most certainly stand in need of redemption of sinful actions that estrange them from God, their neighbors, and themselves. At the same time, their sinful actions have evil consequences that others, and they themselves, have to undergo, and these also cry out for redemption. The situation that needs one sort of redemption generates a situation that cries out for the other sort.

At the same time, people actively sin in some particular circumstances. As often as not those concrete circumstances are themselves evil situations that, having befallen them, distort and break their lives. Those circumstances are the conditions of their sinning, not the consequences. It is not necessary to claim that the circumstances in which people sin excuse them of responsibility for that sin in order to acknowledge that, however much their sinning requires redemption, their circumstances do also. Conversely, people who undergo the most horrendous suffering, if they are not destroyed by it, must respond to that suffering in some fashion. If they respond in sinful ways, then, once again, a situation that needs one sort of redemption has become the occasion of the need of redemption of the other sort also.

In Western Christianity, the two sorts of things that require redemption become most thoroughly intertwined in the situation pointed to by the theological symbol "original sin." Original sin is a change in one's fundamental orientation so that at the deepest level one is turned away from God, estranged from God by one's own act, for which one is responsible and bears guilt. This estrangement is a change each person causes in herself or himself, and it brings with it a massive distortion of human life. Such estrangement and distortion is one sort of thing that needs redemption. At the same time, original sin distorts the human situation before one is born into it. It is an evil that befalls us simply by our being born into a shared, public human world. It is thus also the second sort of thing that needs redemption, an evil that befalls us. It is in the situation of original sin that the two sorts of need for redemption most densely interpenetrate and remind us that in actual life each is always entangled with the other.

Because Christian talk about redemption tends to focus on concrete persons in concrete circumstances rather than on the human scene as such, "redemption" will always be talked about in connection with persons and situations that require both sorts of redemption. At the same time, the distinction between the two is an invaluable tool to use in sorting out different aspects of concrete situations that are in need of redemption and, correlatively, in sorting out different senses of "redemption."

Accordingly, our attempt here to understand the redemptive difference Jesus can make must be focused on particular cases in which we concretely distinguish between the two sorts of redemption. When we ask, "What (redemptive) difference can Jesus make here?" *here* has to be analyzed in terms of that distinction. What *redemption* will mean in the concrete will be relative to the particularities of both the actions concrete people do and the evils that befall them.

This does not yet say what *redemption* itself means. But it does tell us that if talk of redemption is going to count as typically Christian talk it must be framed in a way that makes it clear that, whatever *redemption* turns out to mean, it has to do either with sinful things human beings do or with evils they undergo, and almost never the one without the other.

This last point brings with it one very important implication. What *redemption* means is relative not just to the concrete particulars of persons and situations in need of redemption but also to whether those situations have been created by what the persons themselves did or whether they are situations that simply befell them. Either way, Christianly speaking, there are many "meanings" of *redemption*. These various meanings are not unrelated to each other and, in fact, bear resemblances, but they cannot be dissolved into one omnibus "basic meaning." Moreover, the range of ways that people may do evil and the range of situations in which they may undergo evil is open-ended. In this regard there appear to be no limits either to human inventiveness or to history's novelties. Accordingly, the range of meanings of *redemption* is also open-ended.

For that reason I consistently write not about *the* meaning of redemption, but about *some meanings* of redemption. It would be absurd to claim to be able in the abstract to identify and classify all the possible meanings of redemption, so I can only hope to address some of the meanings. Indeed, I will explore only those relative to one particular sequence of horrendous situations that befell one family; I do not explore meanings of redemption relative to sin that family members most surely committed. In that respect, I will explore only one type of situation in need of redemption, isolated from the other and thus from the full complexity of actual life. My decision to limit the discussion in this way is, of course, arbitrary; but, given the open-endedness of the range of meanings of redemption in concrete human life, such arbitrariness is unavoidable.

5. Redemption tends to be understood temporally. God relating to redeem takes time. More exactly, Jesus makes a redemptive difference only through the movement of time, often lots of time. That time begins here and now on earth. Thus it is a theological commonplace to speak of "the history of redemption." I develop this point a bit in chapter 2.

For now it is enough to note that our attempt to understand the redemption of situations of horrific suffering undergone by certain people has to be framed in terms of God relating to us redemptively now, in this world on earth. No doubt, Christianly speaking, Jesus makes a redemptive difference hereafter as well, and historically most Christian reflection on redemption has concentrated on just that. However, our talk about God's eschatological consummation of creation ought not to be limited to reflections at funerals about life after death and after history. Given the odd way in which God relates to redeem, we must ask about the meaning of redemption in terms of the inauguration of God's long-promised end time on earth now. So we will focus on the question "What *earthly* redemptive difference could Jesus make here?"

But this still does not say what *redemption* itself means. It only tells us that if our talk of redemption is going to count as typically Christian talk about redemption it must be framed in a way that brings out the fact that, whatever *redemption* means, it comes upon us now on earth as something God brings through a period of time. That rules out the picture that redemption grows out of resources we already have in hand, either because we have developed them ourselves, or because the past has brought them to us unbidden.

SOME SENSES OF "REDEMPTION"

Thus far I have been generalizing about ways in which Christians typically talk about redemption without reference to their cultural context. However, Christian communities are always located in the contexts of larger host societies and their cultures, and as participants in those host cultures, members of communities of Christian faith also engage in practices that make up the common life of these larger societies. And as we have noted earlier, some of the practices that make up the common life of Christians' host culture, at least in North America, also involve using *redemption* and related words.

The ways that Christians talk about redemption in the common life of communities of Christian faith and the ways they talk about redemption in the common life of their shared North American culture intersect and influence each other. I suggest that it will illuminate our exploration of what "redemption" means Christianly speaking if we take note of some of those practices in which "redemption" is used in the common life of North American culture.

Everyday English usage is ruled by English grammar, not by Christian theological beliefs. In ordinary, nontheological English we use the words *redeem, redeeming,* and *redemption* in at least three broadly distinguishable ways. The context of each usage is a different set of practices. I suggest that when any of these words are used in a specifically Christian context, to speak of God relating redemptively to the human scene, their ordinary meaning is metaphorically extended in one of three ways that I shall label, respectively, (1) making up for a bad performance, (2) redeeming from alien control, and (3) making good on a promise.

Making Up for a Bad Performance

One way in which *redeem* and related words are used in colloquial English is in connection with the performance of a wide variety of practices. We speak of someone redeeming a poor performance or poor behavior in the past by superior performance or behavior in the present. A baseball batter who has struck out several innings in a row redeems himself by smashing a home run that drives in three runners. A spouse who has forgotten several birthdays and wedding anniversaries is said to redeem himself by remembering the next one with a magnificent bouquet of roses and a bottle of champagne. A criminal whose violence and drug trade have damaged many people is said to redeem himself when, upon release from prison, he trains to become a drug counselor.

This is also, I think, the sense in which the word *redemption* is usually used in the reviews of fiction, theater, and film that I mentioned earlier. These reviewers, writing in nonreligious contexts, find it illumines the artistry of certain kinds of works of narrative art to ask whether the plot of a given narrative includes at least the possibility that no matter how bad earlier performances by the central character or central situation may have been, they may "make up for" them, or be redeemed, by the end of the narrative. What these uses of *redemption* have in common is that they involve making up for earlier bad performances—redemption as making up for bad situations. Similarly, one way redemption is Christianly spoken of is by a metaphoric extension of this everyday English usage. God is said to relate redemptively when God in some way "makes up for" the world's bad performances.

Redemption from Alien Control

Redeem and related words are also used in colloquial English in practices that have to do with borrowing money. Money lenders ordinarily require that the borrower sign over to the lender some valuable property as collateral for the loan. There is an agreed rate of interest on the loan and an agreed time by which the loan will be repaid with interest. During that time the property yielded as collateral for the loan is the property of the borrower but temporarily alienated from him or her and under the control of the lender. If the borrower fails to repay the loan at the rate of interest and within the time agreed, the collateral becomes the lender's property. If the borrower repays the loan as agreed, however, he or she is said to "redeem" the collateral. Closely related is the practice of pawning a possession for money. The pawnbroker holds the pawned object as security until the loan is paid with interest. If the borrower fails to repay the loan as agreed, the pawnbroker may sell the pawned object. If the borrower does repay the loan as agreed, however, he or she is said to "redeem" the pawned object from the control of the pawnbroker.

In such practices, "to redeem" means that the redeemer "regains possession of something in exchange for a payment." For that which is redeemed, "to redeem" has the force of being freed *from* control by some power other than the owner. Let us call this redemption in the sense of "redemption from." Thus another way that redemption is Christianly spoken of is by metaphorically extending this colloquial English use of the word in certain financial practices: God is said to relate redemptively when God frees persons and situations from oppressive powers that bind and distort them.

A Promise Made Good

A third way that *redeem* and related words are used in ordinary English is related to various marketing practices with which we are all familiar. Sometimes, for instance, a manufacturer includes a voucher with a product that the buyer can "redeem" for a cash rebate. Retailers also regularly distribute coupons that can be submitted to the cashier at the checkout counter and "redeemed" for a discount on certain products. And in the 1950s small retailers participated in a practice in which they gave customers "trading stamps" worth a fraction of a percent of their purchases. These stamps, bearing the logo of a trading stamp company, were pasted in a booklet that, when filled, could be "redeemed" for a variety of kinds of merchandise at centers operated by the trading stamp company. The trading stamp scheme attracted customers to the retailers who issued the stamps, and in turn the retailers paid the trading stamp companies a fee to participate. One consequence was that small cities and large towns across America boasted storefronts that displayed a somewhat unsettling sign that read "Redemption Center."

In ordinary English *redemption* has also been used in connection with certain monetary systems. When the United States was on the gold standard, for example, its paper money could be "redeemed" for gold at federally chartered banks. What these practices have in common is this: In each of them a promise is made good. Coupons, vouchers, trading stamps, and paper money, though in themselves nearly valueless, are implicit promises of something else of significant value. When they are "redeemed," it is the implicit promise that has been redeemed.

This use of *redeem* can be generalized. A spoken or written promise, though made of the exhaled air of mere words, explicitly promises something of significant value when it is fulfilled. Its actual fulfillment is the redemption of an explicit promise. Call this "redemption" in the sense of "fulfillment of a promise." A third way then that redemption is Christianly spoken of is a metaphoric extension of this colloquial English use of the word in marketing practices: God is said to relate redemptively when God actually makes good on a promise God has explicitly made to humankind.

Redemption as "making up for"; redemption as "redemption from"; redemption as "fulfillment of a promise": each of these ordinary English phrases has a religiously extended use by Christians. These metaphorical extensions illustrate the intersection of Christians' use of this family of words in practices they share with non-Christian neighbors in the larger culture as well as in practices that make up the common life of their communities of Christian faith.

Distinctively Christian uses of *to redeem, redeeming, redemption,* and related words do not just replicate their use in colloquial English. As we noted above, various features of Christian talk of redemption constrain how this family of words is used in the context of the practices that make up the common life of Christian communities, giving each a peculiarly Christian sense of "redemption." We have seen that, Christianly speaking, "redemption" does not have a single meaning. Although there may well be additional senses of "redeem," for the purposes of this book we will confine ourselves to the three that I have identified in everyday English uses of this set of words. It will make for greater clarity if we keep the word's senses distinct. To avoid muddling them together, I explore each of them in a separate chapter.

2

Promising Contexts

Christian talk of redemption often involves extending metaphorically the ordinary English senses of the word. In colloquial English, for example, the word *redemption* is often used to describe improvements in performances that are considered to have been poor or bad. These performances may be athletic, such as that of a batter who has struck out several innings in a row; or musical, such as a mediocre performance of a particular piece; or moral, such as a criminal action that hurts many people. The people engaged in these performances are seen as redeeming themselves when they subsequently perform in an extraordinarily excellent way that "makes up for" their previous poor performance.

Christians use the word *redemption* and related words in relation to practices that make up their common life as Christians. In the specific sense of "making up for" the word *redemption* is more appropriately used in the context of practices by which Christians struggle to live through horrendous situations and profound suffering than in the context of sins they have committed. Redemption in the sense of "making up for" is invoked in response to the question "What earthly difference can Jesus make *here?*" when "here" is a horrific situation like the AIDS epidemic; or the firebombing of a city such as Dresden, Coventry, or Tokyo; or a child's catastrophic illness. What needs to be redeemed in such situations is not something done by the persons involved but something that has overtaken them. It is not their own poor performance that needs to be redeemed; rather, it is as if the world's own bad performance needs to be "made up for."

Our theological task, therefore, is to imagine what could count as "redemption" by Jesus in the sense of "making up for" the distortion and loss created by such horrendous situations.

FOCUSING THE QUESTION

All horrendous situations and the suffering in which they are experienced are both similar and unique. They are similar in the spiritual, intellectual, and emotional challenges with which they confront us. At the same time, each is unique in its concrete particularity and, correlatively, in what could count as *its* redemption.

Accordingly, in this book I sketch one awful sequence of concrete situations and focus our question on it: What earthly difference could Jesus make here? There is nothing special about this particular horrendous situation. You will know similarly terrible stories, either firsthand or from friends. I have not selected this one because it is in some way "worse" than all the others. It is not. Indeed, it is absurd to suppose that such stories can be ranked and graded as to their horrendousness. In its concrete particularity each is simply what it is, incommensurable with other terrible situations. I focus on this one sequence of situations solely because it is one I happen to know especially well.

This story shares one feature with some, but certainly not all, such stories that makes it an appropriate focus for our effort to answer my friend Milton's question about redemption. Milton asked his question in the context of practices that are part of the common life of communities of Christian faith. My exploration of possible answers to Milton's question speaks out of the same context, and I presuppose a community of persons who engage in practices in which they already do use "redemption" Christianly and, like Milton, want to be clearer about what it means to speak that way.

What makes the story I am about to tell an appropriate focus for this exploration is that it concerns a family that was actively involved in a church. The parents had grown up in families that had been deeply shaped for generations by the common life of Christian communities. When in retrospect these parents ask concerning the events that happened to their family, "What earthly redemptive difference can Jesus make here?" they ask it out of their engagement in the common life of a community of Christian faith. They do not ask it as outsiders longing to be persuaded to identify with such a community nor as skeptics challenging the community's convictions about redemption with powerful counterevidence.

Here is a brief, unadorned, and selective chronicle of events that happened more than a quarter-century ago in the family of a man and woman I know. I did not know the man particularly well at the time, though I have come to know him a bit better since. He was an academic; she, a part-time secretary. They were both in their early forties. They both had lifetimes of active involvement in churches. They had two daughters and a son and lived in a suburb where they were active in a local church and where the children went to public school.

The devastating event I describe and the horrendous situations that followed in its wake center on their son, their youngest child. We'll call him Sam. He was a sweet kid as a second-grader, mischievous, a bit tentative in his interactions with other children. From his father's perspective he was remarkably close to his next older sister. They had the same set of playmates in the neighborhood, and she had always looked out for him. He did well enough in school, but he hadn't quite got the hang of being on his own in school and on the playground.

On the Friday of a Fourth of July weekend, less than two months before his eighth birthday, Sam was diagnosed with pneumonia. Late the next night his father discovered that Sam's breathing had become very labored and that his face was bluish. The clinic instructed them to bring him right in. By the end of the fifteen-minute drive Sam was not moving. They were greeted by a pediatrician and several nurses with a portable oxygen tank. The physician immediately ordered the child transferred by ambulance to the hospital emergency room.

At the emergency room they were met by a resident, an intern, and nurses who attempted to get Sam breathing again on his own. Failing that, they hand-pumped oxygen into his lungs and whisked his gurney onto an elevator. The parents waited for hours in the emergency room, praying that Sam would live. At about three in the morning a doctor came down to say that on the way up on the elevator they had had to perform an emergency tracheotomy and connect Sam to a respirator. He was in a coma.

At first the medical team couldn't diagnose Sam's problem. By a miracle of diagnostic good luck, however, there happened to be present a physician knowledgeable about a rare paralysis whose symptoms she recognized in Sam, although Sam's case was anomalous in several respects. He had the Guillian-Barre Syndrome, characterized as an ascending paralysis. To the lay eye its effects look like those of polio. Perhaps virally caused, it is a disease in which the autoimmune system attacks the nervous system, and it is often preceded by respiratory disease. It leads to paralysis that begins in the extremities, ascends the limbs to the trunk, and then may ascend the trunk. In time, it always recedes, often completely so that the patient is left with only some muscular weakness. Sam's case was anomalous, first in that the disease typically strikes young adults, not children, and second in its extent. Where it typically moves no higher than the chest, Sam's paralysis ascended his complete body so that he could not so much as blink his eyelids or wince.

Sam was in the pediatric intensive care unit for almost four months, three of them in coma, before he was able to breathe on his own again. During that time the only organic system in Sam's body that worked on its own was his circulatory system. Every few hours for three months, day and night, a technician took a blood sample from Sam by which his blood gases could be monitored. The procedure must have hurt, but in his paralysis Sam could not cry out or so much as grimace.

Every day for four months his parents took turns sitting by his bed in six-hour shifts. Those same hours, of course, were hours taken away from being with their daughters. The doctors thought it was possible that he could hear, so they read and talked to him and played cassettes of his favorite songs. On two separate occasions one of them discovered that Sam's respirator had quit working.

As expected, Sam's paralysis began to recede in the third month. When he could breathe on his own, he could sit in a chair, but because of his prolonged inactivity he had lost all muscle tone and had to be strapped in. Once he could talk again, it was clear Sam wasn't Sam. The neurologist characterized his condition as an organic psychosis that would pass, and it did, but it took a month for that to happen.

For the next seven months Sam was in a pediatric rehabilitation hospital learning to walk again and to use his fingers, hands, and arms. The hospital was in a more distant town, and his parents and sisters could get there to see him only on weekends and one evening a week. Sam smiled a lot when his family was around, but it was clear that he was enormously irritable and angry. And Sam had a lot to be angry about. His principal mode of communication had become a string of jokes, teasing remarks, taunts, and insults, after which he'd laugh and say, "Just kidding." On the Fourth of July weekend, exactly one year after he fell ill, Sam was discharged from the rehab hospital.

A child's acute illness is always a terrible event. Each case is terrible in its own way. So what would count as "redemption" of this event?

A series of horrendous situations followed this horrific year. I will describe just one now. Sam was unmanageable at home and at school, and endlessly antagonistic in his relations with other children, his siblings, and his parents. An immensely talented third-grade teacher in Sam's school tried heroically to include him in her class and accommodate both his temperament and his needs, but Sam's power to disrupt the class was formidable. So, at the school system's recommendation, Sam was transferred to a small, private day school that specialized in working with children with serious, neurologically based behavior difficulties. Sam's extreme short-term memory loss and very short attention span intensely frustrated his efforts to learn basic mathematical and reading skills. He could read fluently, but two minutes later could not remember what he had read.

Despite regular work with child psychiatrists for three years, Sam had no positive behavioral changes. Psychological tests showed that he had suffered quite subtle types of brain damage, perhaps from oxygen deprivation. In addition to academic problems, he had difficulty interpreting other people's responses to him. He was completely unable to recognize, for example, that he wasn't being "funny" but was, instead, infuriating everyone with whom he interacted. His acting out at home and in school grew more threatening as he grew physically stronger.

The strain on the family was overwhelming. Sam's sisters, entering early adolescence, withdrew from the family's common life into their rooms or into their friends' lives and families. Their father was emotionally unavailable to them. Above all, he was gripped by the particular fear that is specific to feeling trapped.

As if that were not enough, in the late winter of the third year after Sam returned from the hospital, his mother suffered a psychotic break. She was characterized as suffering major depressive disorder, with possible signs of psychosis and paranoia. She was hospitalized for three months. In the first weeks home from the hospital she was deeply depressed. The father was unable single-handedly to cope with both Sam and his wife, manage a household, parent his daughters, and manage his academic responsibilities. The caseworker from the state's Department of Children and Youth Services and he agreed that Sam needed to be placed in a residential school specializing in children with severe behavioral problems.

By this time it seemed clear that not only was the Sam who came home from a year in hospitals not the child the family had known for almost eight years; he was also never going to be that child again. It was far from clear whether he would ever be capable of normal social relationships, ever be able to acquire more than a third-grade education, ever mature into a self-reliant, self-sustaining adult. Given the family's limited resources of emotional energy, time, and money, what was this terrible event going to do to the future of these people? In his despair, the father, who had prayed fervently that their son's life be spared, lived with intense feelings of guilt and shame at finding himself wondering whether it would not have been better had Sam died.

What earthly difference could Jesus make here?

COPING AND BEING REDEEMED

Let's be clear. The question is not how Jesus might help this family cope. Being empowered to cope with a terrible situation may lead into the situation's redemption, but redemption is supposed to involve more than receiving assistance with one's coping and acquiring coping skills.

Sam's family did receive a great deal of assistance in coping from professional practices highly valued in their urban North American culture. Singly and in various combinations family members worked privately with skilled psychiatrists, social workers, and clinical psychologists. In addition, they had assistance from their local school system and from their state's Department of Children and Youth Services.

The larger community of Christian faith and its faith traditions were also a strong resource. Years of nurture and education by churches had given Sam's father a framework of intellectually rich ideas and emotionally powerful images that deeply shaped his emotional, intellectual, and spiritual responses to what was happening to his son, his wife, and their family. He was at first numb, neither feeling nor thinking beyond what was required just to get through the demands of each part of each day. When the deafening internal noise of anxiety began to subside a bit and he gained enough perspective on his context to identify some of his feelings and formulate thoughts, he became aware that he had a lot of questions about where God was in all of this. He took to rereading Job, with whom he could only partially identify. He was aware of feeling very sad, generally anxious, fearful about several specific matters, and close to despair at being trapped by the likely long-range consequences of Sam's illness. What puzzled him was that, unlike Job, while he knew that there was a great deal to be angry about, he was not aware of feeling particularly angry. He couldn't believe that at some level he was not deeply angry, and he knew how dangerous it is simply to swallow such feelings. But initially he did not feel anger.

Apparently he was not the only one concerned about his well-being. Individual encounters with fellow Christians, some of whom he did not otherwise know, were instrumental in helping him cope, whether they knew it or not.

One day, for instance, while he was sitting by Sam in the Pediatric Intensive Care Unit, Sam's father was told by a nurse that one of the neurologists wanted to talk with him in a nearby conference room. The neurologist, whom Sam's father had never seen before and never saw thereafter, introduced himself, chatted a bit about how unusual Sam's case was and how hard it must be on the family. Then he asked Sam's father if he was religious. Not knowing quite how to answer that, Sam's father simply said that he was a Protestant Christian. The neurologist acknowledged that he didn't know what he could say helpfully as a neurologist, but thought he might have something helpful to say out of his cultural background. As Sam's father could probably tell from his name, he said, his home was in a region of South Asia where the traditional culture was deeply Buddhist. His native culture had values and practices that might be relevant and helpful to Sam's family. There followed a leisurely, though not long, conversation about such values as detachment and various practices of breathing and exercise that nurture detachment.

By the end of the conference, Sam's father was aware that he felt a good deal calmer and more relaxed. What mattered to him even more was his gratitude to this doctor, who had no professional obligation to his son or to him, for taking time to offer him some emotional and spiritual sustenance.

The gratitude turned to amazement several days later when he learned that, in addition to being a distinguished neurologist, this doctor was an ordained Christian minister. The father was amazed at the care with which the doctor had thought through their conversation. Had he engaged Sam's father with talk about implications of their shared Christian faith for the family's situation, the chances were that the conversation would have been so familiar to the father that he would scarcely have heard it. By entering the conversation obliquely in terms of a religious tradition with which the father was unfamiliar, the doctor stood a much better chance of engaging him. The father's amazed awareness that a fellow Christian, a complete stranger, had taken this much care to be with him, in the midst of this family crisis, was, by itself, the sort of thing that could help strengthen him to cope more effectively.

Another day, in the first week of Sam's coma, the family's pastor, unable to gain admittance to the Intensive Care Unit, sought out the father in the hospital cafeteria at lunchtime. The pastor asked about how Sam was doing, how his sisters were dealing with Sam's illness, and how the parents were coping. In particular he "listened actively" to the father's account of how *he* was doing. As the father remembers it, he responded openly, giving a full account, even-keeled, thoughtful, emotionally level though not flat. The exchange was nondirective and professionally pastoral. As they were leaving the cafeteria, the pastor suddenly erupted, smacking his hand hard on the hallway wall, and said loudly to the father, "I don't know about you. If it were my kid I'd be so mad at God I'd pound my fist into this wall."

The outburst jolted Sam's father. At first he was depressed, feeling that he had just been shown to be an emotionally inadequate father. Then it jolted him into a fresh awareness of himself. He realized how he differed from his pastor. To him the idea of being angry at God for what had happened to Sam was simply ludicrous. For better or worse, the framework of Christian ideas and images that shaped his response to Sam's illness totally excluded the idea that God had anything to do with Sam's becoming ill. Among his most primitive religious convictions was that God did not "send" or "cause" such a thing, though God could be trusted to be in some way present to Sam and to the family in the midst of it. He did not think or feel about God the way his pastor did. He was quite comfortable with the idea that ultimately there might not be any answer to the question why this had happened to Sam; the occurrence of evil might well be inexplicable in principle. He realized that the tragedy of Sam's illness had not generated anything like a crisis of faith for him.

At the same time he realized that the fact that he was not angry at God, or at anything else in particular, did not mean that he did not feel angry. There was no reason why anger could not be as free-floating as anxiety, not focused on any particular object. Perhaps it was not true that he did not feel anger. Maybe he had failed to identify feelings he did have as free-floating anger feelings, confusing them, perhaps, with diffuse feelings of anxiety or desperation. The pastor's outburst had jolted Sam's father into an awareness of ways in which he was indeed intensely and appropriately angry about what had happened to Sam, and it did so in the context of the framework of Christian images and ideas he brought with him into this situation. That realization allowed him also to recognize that acknowledging anger before God was not the same thing as expressing anger at God, which continued to feel like a meaningless and ridiculous thing to do. It also led him to recognize that asking Job's questions of God on behalf of Sam could be one way of being faithful to God in the midst of this awful situation, rather than a way of blaming God for this terrible story. Thus here too a brief encounter with a fellow member of the community of Christian faith helped strengthen Sam's father to cope more effectively with the situation.

The congregation to which the family belonged also helped them cope. In large part that help meant such familiar gestures as the delivery of a steady stream of hot meals to the family. The family was sustained not so much by their own faith as by the faith that held that community together—a faith that allowed the community to hold Sam's family up. The community's weekly experience of being held before God in prayer during common worship was also powerfully sustaining for them all.

The community of Christian faith and practice that helped this family cope was larger, of course, than their own congregation. On Sundays the father took the morning shift sitting beside Sam's bed in the Intensive Care Unit, generally leaving for the hospital earlier than the family's congregation held its service. His route to the hospital took him past a church that had an early service, and he began to stop there to worship. The family was unknown to that congregation, and the father knew neither its clergy nor any of its congregants. So he was stunned one Sunday in the second month of Sam's coma to hear Sam prayed for by name during the prayers. He discovered later that one of Sam's physicians, a resident in neurology, was also a congregant and had been so distressed by Sam's illness that she had requested prayer for him. Not only was this a profoundly moving experience, but the knowledge that a larger anonymous community of faith regularly prayed God's care for his son and his family, whom they did not know, was also a powerful support in helping Sam's father cope with what the family was going through.

All the same, help in coping, whether secular or churchly, is not the same thing as redemption. Christianly speaking, we need to be very cautious about characterizing such help as "redemptive" and in particular, must be even more cautious in characterizing the church as a "redemptive community." Christianly speaking, it is only God, definitively described by the story about Jesus, who can redeem; the church and the "helping professions" cannot.

Communities of Christian faith are called not to redeem but to minister. A major part of their ministry is helping people cope with the evils they have to undergo. The purpose of that part of the church's ministry is to prop us up, to keep us standing and moving so that we are "there" and available for God to relate to us redemptively. This ministry is, in the root sense of the word, the ministry of *comfort*, a word that derives from the Latin *confortare*, "to strengthen." It is accurate to say that the church's ministry of comfort aims to "strengthen" or "empower" persons to cope with what befalls them. However, while the church's help with coping may lead people into redemption, it is not the same thing as God relating to redeem.

Another, more basic part of the church's calling drives the ministry of strengthening people to cope with whatever they undergo. This is the church's call to proclaim the good news that, in Jesus, God does in fact redeem horrendous situations. When Christians proclaim that, they seem to be promising something more than resources by which to cope with those situations. What is that "more"?

GOD'S PROMISE IN AN UNPROMISING WORLD

One way that divine redemption is more than help with coping can be imagined by reflecting on the idea of God making a promise to humankind.

The world is so ambiguous that it does not seem to be a very promising or reliable context for human life. Despite the abundance of earth's resources and its ravishing beauty, it regularly visits all manner of violence on its citizens, including situations like those that befell Sam's family. In this it "performs" poorly as a context for human life. In particular, the world that is the context of Sam's family is anything but promising. They have lost the seven-year-old Sam they knew and live with a stranger they cannot handle. They are losing each other as a family.

In large part, the context in which Sam's family lives is colored by their nostalgia for a lost world they had constructed for themselves. It was a world in which Sam and his sisters would excel in school, go off to college, make good friends, find a rewarding life work in which they would distinguish themselves, and, in the process, become their parents' adult friends. Of course, that world was not in reality very promising because Sam's parents had constructed it out of half-truths and illusions. Their nostalgia for it is thus another self-deception. Yet, for all its unreality, that remembered world defines the world in which they have lived since Sam's illness, so that their present world is simply the negation of their nostalgically remembered world. Their remembered world had promised a lovely future; they experience the world they are in now as a trap. They are trapped in it not merely by the terrible things that are really going on in their family, awful as they are, but even more by the illusions and half-truths out of which they constructed the world they lived in before all this overtook them. Especially now, their lived world is anything but promising.

As the Gospels' narratives tell it, Jesus comes into just such unpromising worlds as God's promise of new creation. In the Gospels' stories Jesus comes as a teacher. However, a century of New Testament scholarship has made it plain that the burden of his teaching was not so much a set of moral principles as this *promise:* God's longed-for eschatological end time is about to break into your world. Moreover, in the very way in which the Synoptics tell the story, Jesus not only speaks the promise but, in his person, *is* the promise.

As we noted in chapter 1, it is characteristic of Christians to talk of God's relating redemptively to the human scene through the movement of time. If we now imagine God's redemptive relating to us as God's making a promise to us, then that promise making must also be imagined as something that happens in and through the movement of time. If the mere presence of Jesus' person is God's promise, then God's act of promise making takes time—at least Jesus' lifetime. Actually, in order to take the time of Jesus' life, God's act of promise making must take even longer than Jesus' life.

As Christians have read the Old Testament, God repeatedly made a promise across Israel's history through the prophets. That promise was made in quite general and open-ended ways and about a time in the indefinite future. It had come to be understood as the promise of a blessing on humankind at the end of history, an end-time or "eschatological" blessing. In his teaching Jesus repeats the promise again, but this time about a more specific future. Jesus proclaims that God's eschatological promise will arrive imminently. Furthermore, Jesus' promise, though hardly detailed, is somewhat more specific than the promise had been in the past: the eschatological "kingdom of God," God's ultimate triumph over powers of evil, will be marked by humankind's liberation from bondage to powers of evil and will be the rule of justice and peace. God's promise making in and through the person of Jesus takes the entire time from the prophets' general and open-ended promises through Jesus' birth, his ministry of teaching and healing, and his crucifixion and resurrection appearances.

It is precisely this temporally extended *fact* of God's making that promise about the future that can be imagined as one way in which God relates to humankind redemptively. The very fact of Jesus' living with Sam's family—seen as God's act of making them a promise—can be imagined as a way that God redeems what Sam's family has undergone. By a metaphorical extension of the way we speak in colloquial English of an unfocused musician "redeeming" a bad performance by bringing transporting beauty to the last movement of an otherwise lackluster concert, the presence of Jesus in Sam's family's history may be imagined as God's redeeming the world's poor performance in their lives.

A caveat before we go further: Understanding redemption as God's "making up for" grievous loss is not the same thing as the fantasy that God will "compensate" for grievous loss. We must resist the temptation to imagine "making up for" as "compensation," after the fashion of the insurance industry's providing "replacement value."

"Redemption" in Christian discourse has to do with the future. "Compensation" in the sense of "replacement value" has to do with the past. "Making up for" Sam's family's losses, in the sense of "replacement" of the losses, would mean returning their situation to the state they enjoyed before they suffered the loss. While a stolen automobile can be "made up for" by using insurance money to buy another of the same value, human beings are unsubstitutable. They have no such thing as "replacement value." Jesus does not come promising that God will turn back history, restoring our innocence in the garden of Eden as though nothing bad had happened in the interim. Rather, as the Gospels present what Jesus proclaims by word and deed and what Jesus undergoes, he simply *is* the promise that something radically new is about to break in.

THE POWER OF PROMISE MAKING TO CREATE NEW WORLDS

Jesus' ministry, understood simply as the fact of God's making the promise of eschatological rule, is the concrete presence of God's wild and unpredictable power to create new life-worlds in the midst of the living death of this family's lived-world. The challenge for us is to conceive of Jesus' "wild and unpredictable power" and to imagine what counts as its creating a "new lived-world."

Whatever its inadequacies, one persistent and important feature of liberal Protestant theology is its vigorous affirmation of the impact of Jesus' power on actual, concrete human lives. From Friedrich Schleiermacher's description of the powerful influence of Jesus' "God-consciousness" in the early nineteenth century to Paul Tillich's account of the "power of New Being" mediated through Jesus as the Christ in the mid-twentieth century, liberal Protestant theology has made the theme of Jesus' redemptive power central to its accounts of God's relating redemptively to humankind through Jesus.

Liberal Protestant theology has interpreted Jesus' redemptive power according to four different models, likening it variously to (1) the power that the direct influence of one religiously creative personality can have on another person's religious life,[1] (2) the power a profound teacher of religious and moral insights can have on others,[2] (3) the power that broadcast of a piece of public news can have on others,[3] and (4) the impersonal power that drives life itself.[4] In each case, the choice of the model is dictated by one's picture of the sort of religious person or religious teacher the historical Jesus was, and each model is helpful in that it suggests a recognizable and plausible sense in which Jesus can be thought of as redemptively powerful.

However, there is a serious drawback to these familiar approaches to understanding Jesus' power to redeem: the Gospel narratives, which communities of Christian faith live with as Scripture, do not adequately support them. They present a figure the burden of whose message is the promise that the world as we know it is about to end and the rule of God's justice is about to begin. Decades of critical New Testament scholarship tend to confirm the generalization that for all of their substantial theological differences, the narratives of the Synoptic Gospels and the book of John render a Jesus who proclaims the imminent inbreaking of God's eschatological "kingdom." He is one whose works of healing show, by their overpowering of evil, that the inbreaking is already beginning even as Jesus speaks. He does teach, but his teachings either make the same point in arresting and indirect ways or draw attention to ethical implications of his message about the imminence of the eschaton. Furthermore, much scholarship supports the literary judgment that the Gospel narratives themselves are structured, in their significantly different ways, to render Jesus as one who not only proclaims the promise of God's eschatological victory over evil but in his person *is* God's promise of just that.

Accordingly, we need to imagine Jesus' power to redeem in ways governed by the act of promise making. We need to explore how the sheer act of promise making can be a model on which we may imagine God's wild and unpredictable power to create new life-worlds in the midst of living death. We may take the practice of promise making, rather than the practices through which one person can be religiously or morally influential on the lives of others, as the model by which to imagine one way that Jesus can make a redemptive difference for Sam and his family.

It can be difficult to tell, of course, whether a promise has actually been made. When someone says, "I'll see you next week," or "I'll call you," or "We'll have dinner next month at our house," it can be difficult to tell whether the remark was an expression of a hope, an announcement of an intention, a momentary and fleeting thought, or a promise. Moreover, even when promises are made, their importance to us can vary significantly. For one thing, the importance of a promise may vary with the personal importance of the person who has made the promise. If a friend's friend with little political influence on city council promises to support your proposed legislation but then does nothing, you may be disappointed; if your friend the mayor does the same thing, you may feel betrayed. If an acquaintance promises to meet you for lunch and breaks the promise it may be annoying; if your beloved does the same thing, it can be heartbreaking.

The importance of a promise will also vary according to how much we value its content. We routinely distinguish between relatively trivial promises, made either to us or by us, and extremely important, even life-changing, promises such as a promise to marry, the promise of the job of one's dreams, a wealthy person's promise to name one sole heir. We tend to break, and accept the breaking of, trivial promises without much distress. We tend to see the breaking of significant promises as moral outrages. Moreover, making a promise may strike us as no more than the utterance of a few words, with little more power than the force of the exhaled air by which it is uttered. It may easily seem that speaking, even if it is the making of a promise, is an unlikely model for Jesus' redemptive power.

However, despite this acknowledged vagueness and the variety of importance of promises, certain structural features characterize all promise making, including promises God makes. These features of promise making help make it a more plausible model for the way that Jesus' presence can make a redemptive difference. The work of philosopher J. L. Austin[5] brings them out in theologically helpful ways.

For one thing, Austin points out, speaking is a physical act that has certain kinds of force. Speaking is just as much a bodily act as taking a step, stamping your foot, waving your hand, or striking a blow. Some acts of speech—Austin prefers to call them "utterances"—have the force of reporting something else. Such reports describe a part of the world, an event, someone's thoughts or feelings, past or present. Other acts of speech, however, have the force not of reporting something but of performing something. Austin calls an utterance with this sort of force a "performative utterance." Austin cites the baptismal formula as an example. When those who preside say, "I baptize you in the name of the Father and the Son and the Holy Spirit," they are not reporting something going on elsewhere, say in their own minds, in the mind of the one baptized, or in God. Rather, by saying something they are literally doing something that makes a change in the world.

Making a promise is another example. In making a promise we perform something; we literally *do* things with words. One of Austin's favorite examples is the marriage vow, whether sacred or secular—"I take this woman to be my lawfully wedded wife." The phrase "I do" does not describe or report anything—not the content of the speaker's thoughts or feelings, either past or present. The act of making this promise is not "mere words," for it has the power to create something new, in this case, a new community and a new social institution—this marriage.

A second structural feature of performative acts of speech, including promises, is that they are uttered in the larger context of established social conventions that include public rules governing how performative utterances are to be made. This feature is what makes it possible for performative speech acts to fail. According to Austin all performative acts of speech are subject to two kinds of failure: abuse and misfire. Promise making, for example, can be abused when the promise maker lacks the thoughts or feelings or the commitment to follow through on the behavior the promise anticipates. For example, if I promise to repay your generous loan but have no intention of doing so, or if intending to repay you, I never get around to it, one cannot say that I did not "really" promise. Nor can it be said that I uttered a false statement when I promised, for I was not making a statement, either true or false, about anything. I was making a promise, doing something with words. However, an unkept promise is an abuse of the act of promise making. On the other hand, a performative utterance misfires if (1) the persons and circumstances involved are not those required by the relevant social conventions; (2) the procedure is not executed by all participants correctly; or (3) it is not executed completely according to those conventions. For example, go back to the wedding I mentioned earlier. If the presider is not ordained clergy, a justice of the peace, or otherwise licensed to perform marriages, or if one of the people being married is already legally married to someone else, or if the marriage ceremony is conducted without benefit of a marriage license, then the promises the couple make to each other misfire. That is, their acts of speech fail to do what they are supposed to do and are void and without effect—the couple is not married. No new community, no new lived-world is created for the couple.

Suppose a performative utterance such as a promise does not misfire and is not an abuse of the practice of promise making; how does it have the power to create a new lived-world? Here a third structural feature of promises as performative utterances is important. A promise, Austin points out, is "self-involving"; it commits *you*, the promiser. More exactly, it commits you both to a person or persons and to doing something, to a course of action. The very act of uttering a promise therefore binds the one who makes the promise both to a project, that is, a course of action, and to another person or group of persons. It creates a society of those to whom the promise is made and the one who makes the promise.

Of course, most of the time the societies created by an act of promise making consist of two people, the one making the promise and the one to whom the promise is made. However, there is no reason why such societies may not be much larger. Their size depends entirely on the size of the population to whom a given promise is made.

Moreover, since it is inherent in promise making that the one who makes the promise is self-committed to a project or course of action that has a goal, then it must also be inherent that the promise maker is committed to exercise of power in an ordered and organized way toward that goal. Action in this world, after all, necessarily involves the exercise of power in an ordered and organized way. The society created by making a promise is structured by such exercise of power. That society is not just an amorphous, intersubjective "community" of like-mindedness and shared feelings but a community structured by various sorts of power that are organized in specific ways. If we understand an "institution" broadly as a community in which various sorts of power (e.g., economic, political, cultural) are distributed and structured in relatively stable ways, then a society constituted by an act of promise making is an institution. Promise making has the power to create social institutions in which the promiser is included.

At the heart of the Christian faith is the claim that God makes promises; thus the previous discussion also applies to God's acts of promise making. The case before us is God's promise of the imminent arrival of the blessing of God's eschatological kingdom. The "performative utterance" by which God makes this promise is at once Jesus' ministry of healing and teaching and his person. The promise is made to all humankind. It has the power to create a new social institution that includes God and embraces all human beings. The apostle Paul calls it a "new creation" in Christ.

What difference can Jesus make in Sam's family's situation? His presence in the midst of the living death of their lived-world is the presence of God's act of promise making by which God promises a new creation. As such, it has the power to place Sam's family and their appalling situation in a new and liberating context. If they live into God's promise, Sam's family will live into that new context. In that context their lived-world can be marked by a genuinely open future that they could not have imagined in the living death of the old world they had constructed for themselves. Jesus' presence is both God's promise of this new world and God's invitation to Sam's family to live into it.

A DIFFERENCE JESUS CAN MAKE

Keep in mind that we are reflecting not on the implications of God's actually making good on that promise but on the mere fact of Jesus' presence in the same world with Sam's family as God's act of promise making. The sheer fact of that promise can make a redemptive difference for Sam's family, I suggest, because it can completely change the context of Sam's family. The promise is not the promise of replacement value for all that they have lost, but rather the promise of a new world constructed by God in which the trap of a world that Sam's parents had constructed for themselves out of half-truths and illusions can be relocated and broken open. Thus the world's bad performance as the context of Sam's life and that of his family can, in a way, be made up for.

The effect of Jesus present as God's act of promise making is like the reversal of the relation between foreground and background in a painting. In the scene defined by Sam's family, after Sam's illness, his family's situation is the background. It both defines and frames the scene, that is, the context of each of the people in it. Within that context, Jesus' presence is accented or foregrounded as God's promise. At the same time, Jesus is present in the scene as one person among many within one-and-the-same context. As we have seen, that context is profoundly unpromising, a living death constructed in part by Sam's family out of illusions and half-truths.

However, if Jesus' presence in the family's life is indeed *God's* eschatological promise, background and foreground are reversed. As God's promise of the imminent inbreaking of God's eschatological kingdom, Jesus' presence places Sam and his family in a new and profoundly promising context. Quite apart from anything else changing, we now must imagine the social institution that is created by God's performative utterance. That is, God's promise to all humankind is the context into which the terrible situation that befell Sam's family is relocated.

Because we initially focused our question about the meaning of redemption on Sam's family, their situation defined both their own context and that of everyone present in their lives, including Jesus. But Sam's family is only one reality among many within a shared context. And if Jesus's presence *is* God's act of promise making, it is *his* presence, not the terrible series of situations that Sam's family has undergone, that defines the context they all share. *It* is their "background" now, their context, and it embraces them. When their context is defined by the presence of God's promise rather than by a profoundly unpromising series of events, it amounts to their having a new context. That new context is what can "make up for" the unpromising context that overcame Sam's family. Whether it does or not depends in part on whether Sam's family lives into God's promise. If they do, they will live into their new context. In that context they may have a lived-world marked by a genuinely open future that they could not have imagined in the living death of the old world they had constructed for themselves. Jesus' presence in the world they constructed is God's promise of this new world and God's invitation to Sam's family to live into it.

Our goal has been to imagine as concretely as possible what redemptive difference Jesus could make here and now in situations crying out for redemption. Because what counts as their redemption depends on the particularities of such situations, I have kept the discussion concrete by focusing on the concrete situations that befell Sam's family. We have relied on metaphoric extension of the everyday English remark that someone redeems a bad performance by "making up for" it to help imagine God's redemption of those situations. According to the witness of Christian faith, in his presence in their world Jesus is God's act of promise making to Sam's family, a divine performative utterance that redemptively creates a new context for their lives, "making up for" their old unpromising context.

However, this way of imaging redemption appears to yield only a *possibility* of redemption, a contingent redemption, a redemption Sam's family may—or may not—"live into." Granted, according to the witness of Christian faith, it is a very concrete possibility: the person of Jesus of Nazareth (scarcely anything is more concrete than an actual human person!). Nonetheless, it is a concrete possibility of redemption, not its concrete actualization. In order to imagine redemption more concretely it will be necessary in chapter 3 to combine the metaphor of redemption as "making up for" with a second metaphor of redemption as "redemption from" and in chapter 4, with the metaphor of redemption as "fulfilling a promise." Relying solely on the metaphor of redemption as "making up for" a bad performance, we can only imagine redemption as a contingent possibility: *If* members of Sam's family live in the trust, witnessed by their own religious tradition, that the person of Jesus simply is God's act of promise making, their lives will be located in a new context, a new creation constituted by God's "performative utterance."

This is where the Johannine gnostic moment lies in the Christian story of redemption. Sam's family doesn't stand a chance of living into the new context constructed by God's promise making in the person of Jesus unless they have a moment of insight concerning the promissory significance of Jesus' earthly ministry, a moment of gnosis, when the light shines in their darkness and they "get it" about God's power for new life that has committed and bound itself to them in promise. Their insight doesn't itself have the power to redeem them; but without insight the invitation won't be accepted, the promise won't be lived into.

In this fashion we can understand one way that Jesus' proclamation, in deed and word, of God's promise might be said to redeem Sam's family's situation. It redeems by "making up" for the world's horrifying performance in Sam's illness and his family's disintegration by mediating the power to create a new lived-world out of their living death. However, such redemption won't just happen to Sam's family. They have to learn to live into that promise. The apostle Paul's words to the Philippians is the word of God to Sam's family and to every horrific situation in its concrete particularity—work out our own salvation:

> *Work out your own salvation* with fear and trembling; for it is God who is at work in you, enabling you both to will and to work for his good pleasure.
>
> (Phil. 2:12b, 13)

3

Fellow Sufferer

We are trying to imagine Christianly the redemption of one series of horrendous situations. Only God can redeem, but the way the Gospels tell it, God redeems in and through what Jesus did and underwent. So our question about the awful situation on which we have focused is phrased this way: "What earthly difference could Jesus make here?"

I talk largely of "imagining" redemption rather than "understanding" or "interpreting" or "conceiving" redemption to respect the concrete particularity of the set of situations to which Jesus may make a redemptive difference. Of course, we seek to understand what the word *redemption* means here. Since there is a long tradition of equating the meaning of words with concepts, when we try to understand the word *redemption* it is natural to say that we seek to conceptualize redemption. Since conceptualizing involves interpreting the concept, it is also natural to say that we seek to interpret "redemption." Although I have no interest in challenging that tradition, I fear nonetheless that routine use of words like *conceive* and *interpret* may suggest that this exploration mainly engages our capacities for abstraction—especially abstraction from the particularities of concrete occasions of horrific suffering and, correspondingly, abstraction from the concrete particulars of the redemption of such situations. I propose to speak instead of "imagining" what redemption of this set of situations might mean. It is by imagination that we try to grasp the whole of something in its singular and concrete particularity rather than by abstracting various aspects of it, concept by concept. Our aim, then, is to imagine what redemption of this one set of concrete situations might mean.

Of course, this effort to avoid one misunderstanding may easily foster another. I am not talking about imagined as opposed to "real" redemption. What we seek to imagine is a real, not an imaginary, redemption of this set of situations. While the verb *to imagine* can mean "to make up" or invent, it can also mean "to grasp a concrete particular as some kind of whole."

What earthly difference can Jesus make here? We are asking this question about a particular set of situations in which a boy we called Sam, his two sisters, and his parents found themselves over a quarter century ago. To recapitulate briefly, just as he turned eight, Sam was totally paralyzed and spent three months on a respirator in a coma. The rest of the year he spent in a children's rehabilitation hospital. He emerged with subtle brain damage, learning disabilities, complex emotional problems, and severe behavioral problems. Under the strain of trying to cope with Sam, the family began to disintegrate. His mother suffered a psychotic break and was briefly hospitalized. At first when she returned home she was very depressed. Because neither the public school system nor his family could manage him, when he was twelve Sam was placed in the first of a series of residential schools that combined academics with programs of behavior modification.

To this story one detail needs to be added, which will become significant later. In his first year home from the hospital Sam began occasionally to suffer seizures. In the residential school in which Sam was first placed, and then in the pediatric psychiatric hospital he entered after his first school determined he was suicidal, he continued to have them. Brain tests showed relevant anomalies, and Sam was placed permanently on anticonvulsant medication. The medical staff, however, could not establish any consistent correlation between those anomalies and seizure episodes. Eventually Sam came to trust his therapist enough to acknowledge that he sometimes faked his seizures. The therapist worked with him to bring the practice to an end, but Sam continued on an irregular basis to fake seizures at each of the residential schools in which he was subsequently placed. In fact, he continues to do so as a middle-aged man, and he is so skilled that even well-trained staff have difficulty distinguishing authentic from faked episodes. It is well known among staff that he does this, and it makes it difficult for them to know how to deal with the episodes they observe.

That is not the end of it. Several weeks after she returned home from her hospitalization Sam's mother's depression lifted enough that she felt she could take a part-time secretarial job. She continued in the care of an able psychiatrist, and she seemed to be managing increasingly well. Then she killed herself.

Twelve-year-old Sam, away at school, was certain that she had committed suicide because she was upset by the bad behavior that, he believed, had caused him to be sent away to school. He began acting out in dangerous ways, was deemed suicidal himself, and was placed in a children's psychiatric hospital. He lived there, attending the hospital school, and was fortunate to have a skillful therapist, until he was fifteen. Their mother's suicide, of course, was also deeply traumatic, if in less dramatic ways, for Sam's two sisters and his father.

What earthly difference could Jesus make to this particular situation? Note that this is not a question about what redemptive difference Jesus could make to sin that either Sam or some member of his family may have committed. The question is what redemptive difference Jesus could make to these situations in which a series of evils befell Sam and his family.

"REDEMPTION FROM"

As we have discussed, Christian talk about redemption metaphorically extends familiar, ordinary meanings of the word *redemption*. In colloquial English *redeem* can mean "to regain possession of something in exchange for a payment," as, for example, redeeming a pawned object or redeeming the collateral for a loan. In this use, "redeeming" something has the force of "freeing it from control by some other power." Let's call this sense of the term "redemption as freeing from." It has been extended in many different ways in Christian discourse to characterize how God goes about relating to humankind in and through what Jesus does and undergoes. Not all of those extensions are helpful in the case of Sam and his family, but one in particular can be helpful in imagining what difference Jesus could make to them.

WHICH JESUS?

Before going further it is important to be clear about who the Jesus is who can make a redemptive difference. I will call him the "God-related Jesus." When we ask *who* someone is, we are asking for a description of that person's unsubstitutable personal identity. An adequate description of who Jesus is would include as essential to Jesus' personal identity the information that he has a uniquely intimate relationship with God whom he called "Father" and that God so relates to Jesus that God works redemptively in and through all that Jesus does and undergoes. Such a description would make Jesus' God-relatedness and God's Jesus-relatedness essential to Jesus' personal identity. If we think of Jesus apart from those relationships, we no longer have in mind the Jesus referred to in our question; we have someone else. As Hans Frei argued in his ingenious and imaginative study *The Identity of Jesus Christ*,[1] just such a description of Jesus' unsubstitutable personal identity in terms of his God-relatedness is offered by the narrative structure and plot of the Synoptic Gospels.

An adequate description of Jesus' personal identity also must note that he lived a particular, concrete human life at a particular time and in particular places. He is in that way a historical Jesus, and many aspects of his life and identity are open to historical research. However, he is not solely the "Jesus of historical research." An identity description of Jesus arrived at only through historical research cannot include God's relation to Jesus as essential to his identity, for the evidence and argument proper to historical research do not claim relevance or competence regarding questions about God and God's relation to anything, including Jesus. A historian's reconstruction of Jesus' identity cannot be turned into a theological identity-description of Jesus by some ingenious methodological move. If God-relatedness is essential to Jesus' personal identity, then an adequate description of who Jesus is must be theocentric from the start. The God-relation cannot be suddenly tacked on at the end of the description as yet one more "fact" about him.

An adequate description of this Jesus would also include as essential to his personal identity the following conclusions: (1) who Jesus is invites persons to respond to him in faith; and (2) many instead are scandalized by him. In that sense he might be said to be the "Jesus of faith." However, he is not a "Jesus of faith" in the sense that persons' responses to him in faith somehow constitute Jesus' personal identity. Other people's faith in him does not make him who he is. Either God's redemptive activity in and through what Jesus does and undergoes is essential to Jesus' personal identity in ways conveyed by the narrative logic of the Synoptic Gospels, or it is not. But in any case, that is independent of people's faith or lack of faith in Jesus.

In chapter 2 we concentrated on one strand of Jesus' identity: Jesus as teacher who promises the imminent inbreaking of God's eschatological rule. We reflected on how that promise making could put the unpromising world Sam's family constructed for itself in a new and liberating context, redeeming their situation by "making up" in a certain way for what they had been through.

Now we concentrate on another strand of Jesus' identity: that of a righteous person, teaching righteousness and promising God's eschatological righteousness, who is unrighteously tortured and crucified. We shift from who he is in his ministry to who he is in his passion.

UNHELPFUL IMAGINING

There are at least three familiar ways, or models, to imagine the difference Jesus in his passion can make for terrible situations like that of Sam and his family: (1) evil as punishment; (2) perfection through suffering; (3) the Fellow Sufferer who understands. Each of them is finally, however, unhelpful to imagining how Jesus could redeem the situations in which Sam's family finds itself.

Evil as Punishment

The traditional view of evil as punishment is widespread in popular Christianity, although I am hard-pressed to name one major Christian thinker who defends it in this form. It reflects a deeply rooted primal response that many people have to experiences of evil, whether their own or that of others: Maybe, so the thinking goes, we (maybe they) are being punished for something. We could speculate on the psychology of this phenomenon. Is it, for example, rooted in widespread, unfocused feelings of guilt fostered by a culture that relies heavily on manipulation of guilt to control behavior? Who knows? What matters is that this sense that the evils that befall us are punishment is widely shared.

This perspective on the redemptive difference Jesus' mission can make for Sam's family imagines the evil and suffering that befall people like Sam and his family in a way that is older than Job and his friends. It imagines evil as punishment for misbehavior according to an unfailing rule by which the degree of punishment is proportionate to the seriousness of the misbehavior. Job's friends were certain that the horrific events Job was undergoing were punishment for sin he had committed. Given that picture, Job's continued insistence on his innocence could only make things worse, for it amounted to adding sin to sin as either (1) a sinful refusal to continue the self-examination that might ferret out the sin for which he was being punished, or (2) a refusal to confess and repent a sin he had identified.

If the evil we experience is imagined as punishment for our sin, then the evil Jesus undergoes in his passion must also be imagined as punishment. However, what Jesus undergoes in his passion cannot be imagined as punishment for Jesus' own sin, for he is held to be sinless. If God works to redeem through what Jesus does and undergoes, then in what he does and undergoes Jesus must be so attuned to God, so united with God in will, mind, and heart that sinful opposition to God or separation from God is unthinkable in him. If Jesus' passion must be imagined as punishment for sin and yet he is himself sinless, whose sin can it be that he is punished for if not ours?

Imagined in this way, in his passion Jesus takes on the punishment that our sins have deserved. He instead of us undergoes the full extent of that punishment. Whatever evil does befall is nowhere near proportionate to the magnitude of our sins. Punishment proportionate to our misbehavior would be unimaginably greater than anything any of us in fact suffers. That our suffering is not more severe is because Jesus suffered what he did in his passion for us. The evil Jesus undergoes in his passion redeems us from the full punishment our sins deserve. It also gives meaning to the evil we do suffer by showing it to be our way of participating in what Jesus suffers. Thus, we can say that Jesus' passion redeems us not only from our sin but also from the evil we undergo, or at any rate from its meaninglessness.

Clearly, this way of imagining redemption of the evil Sam's family has experienced would erase the distinction I have drawn between the redemption of evil the family undergoes and the redemption of the sin they commit. In this picture redemption of evil follows from and depends on redemption of the sin for which the evil was the punishment. Redemption of sin is basic, and both evil and sin are redeemed when sin is redeemed. At bottom the only meaning "redemption" would have, Christianly speaking, would be redemption of the sin Sam's family has committed.

This understanding is entirely unhelpful, I suggest, not just in the case of Sam and his family but in every case of horrific evil undergone by anyone. What happened to Sam's sisters and parents was largely the result of what happened to Sam. It is impossible to imagine that seven-year-old Sam had committed any sins of such seriousness that what happened to him and his family was proportionate punishment. It is even harder to imagine that what happened to Sam and his family was *not* terrible enough to count as "proportionate" punishment, so that Jesus' passion can and must supplement it to redeem them from additional punishment. This way of imagining the redemptive difference Jesus can make simply does not fit them. It is unhelpful to their case to try to imagine how Jesus in his passion can redeem the evil that befell them merely by redeeming the sin they, and Sam in particular, had committed.

Furthermore, the Jesus whose redemptive difference is imagined in this tradition is reported to have explicitly rejected its basic image. In Luke, after Jesus has warned in chapter 12 that the day of final judgment is near and has urged readiness, some present "told him about the Galileans whose blood Pilate had mingled with their sacrifices" (13:1). Although the incident is unknown outside Luke, Galileans had a reputation for sedition, and it would not have been out of character for Pilate to have ordered troops to kill anyone who caused a disturbance at the Temple during a festival in such a way that their blood mingled with their sacrifices. Jesus' listeners seem to have suggested that they felt these victims had deserved this punishment for their sins, for Jesus asks them,

> "Do you think that because these Galileans suffered in this way they were worse sinners than all other Galileans? No, I tell you; but unless you repent, you will all perish as they did. Or

those eighteen who were killed when the tower of Siloam fell
on them—do you think that they were worse offenders than all
the others living in Jerusalem? No, I tell you; but unless you
repent, you will all perish just as they did."

(Luke 13:2–5)

Jesus' listeners seem to have sided against the Galileans and do not
raise the problem of unmerited suffering. Neither does Jesus. Indeed,
in Matthew (13:42, 50; 22:1–13; 24:36–51; 25:14–30, 31–46), and
arguably in Luke (13:22–30), Jesus affirms that judgment will fall on
sin, but he imagines that judgment as an eschatological event and does
not identify it with evils that overtake people during their lives before
the end time. What Luke's Jesus does challenge is the picture that punishment follows sin according to an unfailing rule by which the degree
of punishment is proportioned to the seriousness of the sin. No, the sin
of the Galileans and the sin of those on whom the tower of Siloam fell
was no greater than that of Jesus' listeners. Here Jesus may even be
challenging the very notion that sin can be quantified and compared as
greater or lesser. In challenging the quantifiability of sin and the image
of evils suffered as punishment proportionate to sins done, Luke's Jesus
challenges this entire way of imagining the redemptive difference Jesus
can make in his passion.

Jesus' rejection of this way of imagining evil undergone as punishment for sin is more radical in John. As he walks in the Temple precincts,
according to John 9, Jesus sees "a man who had been blind from birth.
His disciples ask him, 'Rabbi, who committed the sin that caused him
to be born blind, he or his parents?' 'Neither,' answered Jesus. 'It was
no sin on this man's part nor on his parents' part. Rather, it was to let
God's work be revealed in him. . . .'" (9:1–3; trans. Raymond E. Brown[2]).
With that Jesus heals the man's blindness so that he sees.

John's Jesus explicitly rejects the idea that the evil inflicted on the
blind man was punishment for sin. Jesus imagines this evil not in terms
of its cause but in terms of the significance it achieves when God does
what God proposes to do with it. God has the resources, working in
and through what Jesus does in relation to this man, to disclose God at
work redemptively in the healing of this man's blindness. By that healing, the man's blindness comes to signify not past sin but God's
redemptive liberation of the man from permanent darkness. Here

John's Jesus not only challenges the image that is basic to this way of imagining the redemptive difference Jesus can make in his passion, but he also offers an alternative.

The way both Luke's Jesus and John's Jesus challenge this traditional way of imagining the relation between sin and evil and the way Jesus can make a redemptive difference suggest that it has little support in the New Testament.

Perfection through Suffering

The New Testament has a clearer basis for a second traditional way of imagining the difference Jesus in his passion can make for awful situations like those that Sam's family underwent. It is, however, also unhelpful to the situations Sam's family are in. This way of imagining the difference Jesus can make goes as follows: In his passion Jesus is the exemplar for Sam and his family of why God sends suffering. The world is an arena of soul making. Human beings are distorted, impure, imperfect. God sends suffering as part of the process of our redemption from spiritual and moral imperfection, and it is particularly through suffering that human souls are purified and made perfect. The proof text for this has been Heb. 2:10: "It was fitting that God, for whom and through whom all things exist, in bringing many children to glory, should make the pioneer of their salvation [Jesus] *perfect through sufferings.*"

According to this way of imagining redemption, Jesus as pioneer of salvation (read "redemption") is the example of someone becoming perfect through suffering. He shows Sam and his family the point of accepting all that befell them as God's gift. And he shows them how to go through such suffering faithfully.

This tradition has a long history in Christian thought and piety. It received a powerful lease on life in mid-twentieth-century Christian circles through C. S. Lewis's widely influential early book *The Problem of Pain,*[3] especially in the first edition of the book, although subsequent editions toned down the idea. Lewis's thesis comes through a few brief quotations:

> We cannot know . . . that we are acting at all for God's sake, unless the material of the action is contrary to our inclinations, or (in other words) painful. (87)

The . . . self exists to be abdicated and, by that abdication,
becomes more truly self. (140)

The redemptive effect of suffering lies chiefly in its tendency
to reduce the rebel will. (100)

There is something right, I think, about this way of imagining
redemption. There is a "self" that needs to be "abdicated." It is the
"self" that is in mind in Jesus' saying in Matt. 10:39: "Those who find
their life will lose it, and those who lose their life for my sake will find
it." However, it is important that we be as clear as possible about just
what or who that "self" is.

Much of the time for a few of us, and perhaps a little of the time for
all of us, the "self" that we need to lose really is a "rebel" self that refuses
to commit itself to live with God and neighbor in love and insists on
reorganizing the cosmos as though it were God. In 1937 as Hitler's
aggressive ambitions were about to explode in World War II, theologian Emil Brunner characterized this "self" in his book *Der Mensch im
Widerspruch*. *Widerspruch* can be translated as "contradiction," but the
English translation of Brunner's book carried the title *Man in Revolt*.[4]
Brunner depicted sinful human being as in conflict with God. The
"self" that needs to abdicate is the self that revolts against God, willfully challenging God. Aggressively hostile to God, it is God's enemy
that seeks to displace God and usurp God's status and role in reality.

However, the picture that human beings are, as human, inherently
titanic figures storming against God is almost comically overdrawn.
Most of the time most of us are far too confused and indecisive about
what we most want, too passive and self-protective, to fit such a picture. Most of us don't want to storm God, let alone be God; we want
to be inconspicuous enough to keep out of God's way.

More often the "self" that needs to be "abdicated" is an insular self
that is complacently oblivious to the particular reality of other creatures. It is not that it denies that there are other realities than itself. It
is aware that there is that which is "other" to itself, including God, but
it lacks interest in the other realities for themselves. Lacking interest,
it fails to *attend to* the concrete particularity of each "other" as a reality
in its own right that is independent of the "self." Like the first version
of the "self" that must be abdicated, this one is also profoundly "self-

centered." Its self-centeredness, however, is not a willful challenge to God's primacy, an aggressive seeking to substitute itself for God. Rather, it is mindlessly passive, inattentive to other realities and oblivious to the way that, in their particular actualities, they are independent of the self.

To abdicate such a "self" is to learn to pay attention to others' concrete, particular actualities. To learn to pay attention to them in their independence is to learn to love them as they are for what they are. The love that consists of paying attention in this fashion is what novelist and philosopher Iris Murdoch called "perfect love,"[5] "perfect" because it is God's way of loving. As Diogenes Allen has written it in his remarkable meditation in *The Path of Perfect Love*, to love in this way "is to perceive particulars as irreducible realities that are not to be put into orbit around oneself, nor to be made an example of something else, a specimen of a universal. . . . What we are to love is a particular, a center, full of unrealistic worth but also of true worth that is not exhausted or captured by whatever likeness it has to others."[6]

To learn to love in this way is, as C. S. Lewis said, to abdicate the self in both of the senses of "self" that we have distinguished. For it is to learn to love God, thus abdicating the willfully God-hostile "self," and one's fellow creatures, thus abdicating the "self" that is complacently inattentive to others in their particularities.

To learn to surrender that "self," to learn to love with "perfect love," is to undergo a radical change in the basic pattern of one's life. It is, as it were, a change from the Ptolemaic vision of the universe to the actual Copernican model. For Ptolemy the earth lies at the center of the universe and all other realities orbit about it for its benefit. Their significance is defined by that center. Copernicus showed the universe has a quite different pattern: earth is but one of many realities interacting and interrelated in a vast dynamic system that orbits around the sun. The traditional name for such a change in the basic pattern of one's life, of course, is "conversion." It is painful to undergo.

Here lies what is right about the traditional way of imagining the redemptive difference Jesus can make in his suffering and death. Suffering does *accompany* the deep change in the pattern of our lives that comes with redemption. Furthermore, the suffering caused by horrendous events that have nothing to do with a change in the basic pattern of our lives, events in which we "hit bottom," can be the *occasion* for beginning to learn how to attend to others with the attention that is "perfect love" of them.

This point must be made carefully, however. It is one thing to say that suffering regularly accompanies the changes in our lives brought by redemption and to note that deep suffering is sometimes the occasion for starting to learn to attend to others in their particularities and for their own sakes. It is quite another thing to say that suffering *as such* is inherently redemptive. It is simply not true; so it cannot be true that Jesus' passion is an example of the redemptive power of suffering as such. Suffering as such does not necessarily have the power to perfect lives. Suffering can just as well disintegrate people and corrode their relationships. What befell Sam's family did just that to Sam, to his mother, and to the family itself. So, as far as Sam and his family are concerned, we must set aside as unhelpful the story of Jesus' passion as the exemplar of redemption-as-perfection-through-suffering.

The Fellow Sufferer Who Understands

Distinctly modern variations of imagining the redemptive difference Jesus can make in his passion are omnipresent in late twentieth-century, pastorally enlightened, empathic Christian talk. It is generally imagined this way: In Jesus' passion God's self is present among us in the midst of our suffering as—in Alfred North Whitehead's famous phrase—"the fellow sufferer who understands."

Although this perspective is, I think, ultimately unhelpful in imagining what difference Jesus could make in his passion, there is something right about it too. It *is* important to know that someone understands what we are going through. If God's relating to Jesus and Jesus' relating to God are both essential to Jesus' personal identity, then in Jesus' passion God is in some way participating in what Sam and his family undergo. God is in solidarity with them in their suffering. So it can be affirmed to Sam and his family, "God does understand what you are going through; God is going through it with you." Surely that is true. There is something right about imagining Jesus in his passion as the fellow sufferer who understands.

All the same, if left at that, there is also something profoundly inadequate about this way of imagining redemption. As David Tracy some-

where remarks, characterizing God as "the fellow sufferer who understands" risks making God in the image of an Edwardian gentleman
who, stereotypically, is benevolent in a generalized sort of way, with a
sensibility so exquisitely refined that he registers the distress of each
fellow creature, well-intentioned but terminally ineffectual.

To know that your suffering is understood by somebody is deeply
comforting. However, just as redemption is about more than help in
coping with an awful situation, it is also about more than receiving
comfort in an awful situation. To be comforted is to be soothed, calmed,
blanketed in care. It is also to be empowered, strengthened to survive.
If "the fellow sufferer who understands" is the best way to imagine
Jesus' redemptive effect in his passion, then Sam and his family would
be fully justified in responding to the God who works in and through
what Jesus does and undergoes, "Sir, we really appreciate your concern
and your understanding. It does strengthen us to survive. But couldn't
you just help change things a little?"

Redemption is something beyond giving comfort. At least in one
sense of the term, if Jesus in his passion can redeem Sam and his family, it means that through what Jesus undergoes God can regain possession of them from powers that dominate and distort their lives. In
that connection imagining Jesus as the fellow sufferer who understands
does not adequately illuminate how Jesus can make a difference.

JUSTIFYING OUR LIVES

The image of the fellow sufferer can be revised in a helpful way. One
difference the afflicted and crucified Jesus can make for Sam and his
family is to free them from the power that distorts their personal identities in a living bondage. Whether or not one's identity is distorted by
a living bondage turns, I suggest, on how one answers the question
"What makes life worth living?" Correlatively, the way Jesus' passion
can make a difference turns on the same question.

Nothing confronts us with the question whether life is worth living
so forcefully as the suicide of an acquaintance, not to mention the suicide of someone you have loved. Perhaps Sam's mother decided that
her life was not worth living; or, on the other hand, perhaps she was in
no condition to decide anything. In either case, for her children and

husband her death did focus the question "What *does* make this life worth living?"

This is part of what mid-twentieth-century theologian Paul Tillich had in mind in his famous remark that existentialism was the good luck of Christian theology. He meant that the writings of secular, atheistic existentialist philosophers like Jean-Paul Sartre were a boon for Christianity following the Second World War. In his view, this was partly because existentialism, by its broad cultural influence on the arts and cinema, provided a commonly shared language in which it was possible to clarify Christian ideas that otherwise had become obscure or unintelligible to secular people. In particular, Tillich was drawing attention to the fact that many existentialist thinkers focused on suicide as the phenomenon that most sharply brings to the surface of consciousness what they took to be the most important question of all: What makes life worth living?

Of course, now at the beginning of the twenty-first century we don't think about suicide; we deem it a sign of emotional illness to do so. But a suicide does most powerfully focus for us this question: What gives the value to our lives that justifies the time and space we take up living and the consumption of resources that keep us going?

Perhaps most of us answer that question in the following way: A life that has a certain dignity that commands respect is a life worth living, and this respect derives from the quality of things we *do*. In particular, perhaps most of us live trusting—a kind of faith—that our lives will have value and so be worth living *if* we do what a responsible citizen, a productive member of society, a provident parent, a loyal friend, a decent person would do in our circumstances and social roles. Every human society teaches its members a set of such roles, and it also teaches the rules by which to assess the degree of excellence with which they are filled. The closer we come to satisfying the rules, the more excellent is our performance of the roles we take on; the more excellent our performance of the roles, the more clearly valuable our lives. And the more valuable our lives, the more firmly grounded is our sense that, yes, the time and space we take up living is justified; yes, this life is worth living. I am not saying that this is a policy people adopt explicitly, intentionally, and consciously. Rather, I am talking about a pattern and dynamic that persons' lives show whether they are conscious of it or not. It is a pattern that many cultures, and ours in particular, reinforce from earliest childhood onward.

What I am describing here is the idea of living our lives trusting that they are justified by works that satisfy some law. When the apostle Paul inveighed against justification by works of the law, the law he had in mind was quite specifically the Torah. Reiterating the polemic, the Reformers understood the law more broadly as moral law, whatever its source and grounding. In modern Protestant theology the law has been understood even more broadly as any social convention that serves as a criterion of excellent performance.

According to each of these variations on the theme, living in trust that our lives are justified by what we do in accord with standards of excellence lies at the very heart of sin. What we do sinfully need not even be immoral; even if what we do is morally good, it is sin if we trust the doing of it to show that our lives are worth living.

It was the apostle Paul's point that sin, that is, trusting works done in accord with a law to justify our lives, will lead only to a living death. If we define who we are by the excellence of what we do, as measured by a law, our life is in bondage to that law. But, Paul insisted, the law cannot give life because trying to satisfy it perfectly is a never-ending project. If life, that is, the worthwhileness of one's life, depends on completing the project, life is impossible. Only failed life, only living death, is possible.

A second way in which people at least implicitly answer for themselves the question "What makes your life worth living?" also values respect. In this case, people suppose that what shows that life is worth living is that something *about them* commands respect.

One way to gain that respect, frequently derided nowadays, is to define oneself above all as a victim. One lives on the supposition that what justifies the time and space I take up living is the respect I command simply because I have been victimized by some unspeakable evil. This pattern need not be adopted with self-conscious intent; what matters is the pattern to the way people live, whether they are aware of the pattern or not.

Defining oneself as worthy of respect because of one's victimization is sometimes rightly derided because it seems to be a way to wallow in self-pity, to manipulate other people's pity, and to avoid taking responsibility for oneself. Nonetheless, people do adopt this pattern of life because it can evoke the respect that, however briefly, reassures them that their lives are worth living.

Away at school, separated from his family, Sam learned that he could win sympathy and present himself as deserving his classmates' respect and even awe by telling his story as one not only of unique victimization by a frightening disease but even more as one of being abandoned by his mother's suicide. When he lived that way Sam lived on the supposition that what made his life worth living was the respect owed him because of the uniquely terrible things that had made him their victim.

There is another general way in which people seek to show that because their lives command respect their lives are worth living. It shares with the first version only the fact that the people who adopt it have undergone terrible events. In this case, however, what commands respect is not that persons have been victimized but that the horrific events themselves evoke a terrified awe in those who watch or hear about them. Those who pass through such horrific events thus command a certain respect. Their persistence through horrific events and their sheer presence now are in themselves mute testimony to just how terrifyingly horrendous the contexts of our lives can in fact become. That testimony receives deep, inarticulate respect. Consider, for example, the respect accorded Holocaust survivors—respect evoked not by victimization but by survival. Here too the pattern need not be adopted with self-conscious intent. What matters is the pattern to the way people live, whether they are aware of the pattern or not.

Soon enough both Sam and his father were living in different variations of just that pattern. It may be that Sam's sisters did also; however, since I know this story chiefly from the perspective of Sam and his father I can only comment on them. Away at school, separated from his family, entering adolescence and unskilled in relating to his peers, Sam learned to define his identity in terms of the terrible things that had happened to him. He lived his life as though his identity were simply the kid who had that terrible disease, who has that scary tracheotomy scar on his throat, whose mother killed herself. That identity commanded not just pity but a measure of respect that helped counterbalance the enmity he regularly generated by his obnoxious behavior. For his part, Sam's father, overwhelmed by the responsibilities of being a single parent and his apparently unlimited liability before Sam's seemingly interminable dependence on him, lived his life as though his identity were simply the man whose son has suffered this appalling medical history, whose wife has committed suicide, who alone is responsible for caring for his almost unmanageable son for the rest of his life.

On plenty of occasions both of their personal identities were marinated in self-pity, although it would be too simple to say that Sam and his father defined themselves merely as victims. They certainly did in part. However, their personal identities were also defined as survivors of horrific situations. The sheer horror of those situations commanded respect. Both Sam and his father lived on the tacit supposition that that respect underwrote the worth of their lives. This pattern in their lives was just another way to justify the time and space they took up living.

This pattern is not to be confused with the pattern of justifying life by the quality of its achievements. Strictly speaking, the pattern of Sam's life and his father's is only analogous to the pattern of lives seeking justification by works. Granted, to survive a terrible situation is to do something, to perform some sort of work. However, what is at issue here is not bad things done but bad things undergone; not sin, but evil. More exactly, the issue is not the sinful living death of a life of self-justification by works that accord with a standard of excellence, but rather the distortion of personal identity by its bondage to evil endured. Accordingly, our question is not "What difference can Jesus make in regard to their living death in sin done?" but "What difference can Jesus make in regard to their identities distorted by evil undergone?"

THE FELLOW SUFFERER WHO SETS FREE

A problem with defining personal identity in the way Sam and his father do is that it distorts one's identity by binding it to horrible situations in the past. The problem lies not so much with the horror as with the pastness. If what justifies one's life, what shows that it is indeed worth living, is surviving a set of horrendous events in the past, then everything that happens later and everything one does later must be interpreted and shaped by reference to those past events. One's future is defined by, and so is in bondage to, an event in the past.

So, for example, as Sam slowly becomes more capable of intentionally managing his own affairs, he still cannot allow himself to live more autonomously because of *who* he is. He has defined his identity as that of one made dependent on others by his disabilities. When possibilities arise that could expand the range of his life, he leaves them unexplored because they don't fit his definition of who he is. When he gets part-time jobs for which he longs, he sooner or later sabotages himself by faking seizures. Although he wants to work the way everybody else does, and looks forward to the little bit of extra income it brings in, working does not fit his definition of himself as a person disabled by horrendous events. After a certain number of seizure episodes, his employers always have to let him go. Sam also shows some artistic talent. When he is admitted to the town school system's adult education art class, he fakes seizures and is asked not to enroll again. He lives as though he must keep his self-definition as survivor of horrendous events continually in the public eye. His old identity must not be eclipsed by the appearance of a new identity as "ordinary worker" or "talented young adult." As he matures in his ability to make and keep friends Sam does not form a social network for himself, for it is essential to his identity that he is one who has lost family. "Lacking a support system" is part of his identity.

So too with Sam's father. Even when in young adulthood Sam's life is supported and structured by a network of social agencies, his father continues to organize his own life in such a way that everything else is fit around the edges of his perceived responsibilities for Sam—for being endlessly responsible for Sam defines who he is.

Neither of them could imagine or allow any new joyful event, any new creative accomplishment, any new friendship to be *more* definitive of who they are than the terrible events to which their identities have been bound by definition. Theirs are distorted identities, frozen in time and closed to growth.

The difference Jesus in his passion can make to Sam's and his father's distorted personal identities can indeed be imagined in terms of "the fellow sufferer" if we follow the evangelists' description of Jesus' personal identity. They tell the story of Jesus' suffering and crucifixion as at once the story of what a human being did and underwent and as the story of what God does in and through what Jesus did and underwent. It is the story of God's own presence in horrendous situations like the ones Sam and his family were in, of God's solidarity with them, in love for them, in a love that makes itself vulnerable to suffering with them. Essential to Jesus' identity is God relating to Jesus so that God's self is present as fellow sufferer.

It is important to stress that God's fellow suffering in, through, and under Jesus' passion is not just God's way of understanding what we go through. It is God's own odd way of going about loving us, God's concrete act of loving us in the midst of the most terrible circumstances we can go through. It is just *that* love that can redeem personal identities like Sam's and his father's from their distorting bondage to past events, for it is God's love for them that grounds the worth of their lives. Neither the excellence of what they do as measured by some set of rules nor their awesome survival of horrifying events can do that. It is only God's concrete act of loving them in the midst of the most appalling situations that makes their lives worth living. That alone can justify the time, space, and resources they take up by living.

In Jesus' passion God is the fellow sufferer who can redeem Sam and his father from bondage to the past that distorts their personal identities. God's loving them in Jesus' passion is the most embracing context of their lives. That love, not the horrors they have been through, is the context that defines who they are. That context is not defined by any past, but only by God's free and loving creativity in the present. Sam's and his father's identities are opened to the future and freed from bondage to the past when they are defined by that love now.

They have only to live into that context for their identities to be redeemed from imprisonment to the horrendous things they have undergone. They have only to live in trust that it is God's loving them in Jesus' passion that makes their lives worth living. Living in that trust, living into the embracing context of that love, will take time. It is not the trusting that will redeem them from the distortion of their personal identities. It is God's loving them that will do that.

The apostle Paul's words to the Philippians are the word of God to Sam's family and to everyone living in a horrific situation in its concrete particularity, reminding them that it is God who is at work in them:

> Work out your own salvation with fear and trembling; for it is God who is at work in you, enabling you both to will and to work for his good pleasure.
>
> (Phil. 2:12b, 13)

4

Breaking Vicious Cycles

We are trying to imagine Christianly what might count as the redemption of a series of terrible situations in the lives of Sam and his family. We are assuming that, by definition, to imagine redemption Christianly is to imagine redemption as something God does here and now in and through what Jesus did and underwent. So our question is, "What earthly difference can Jesus make to this series of situations that overtake Sam and his family?"

It is important to keep in mind that our question about redemption in this case does not focus on these persons' bondage in the sinning they do, though they certainly stand in need of redemption from that as well. That is an important issue on which to reflect, but at another time and in a different book, one about atonement and reconciliation. Rather, what cries for redemption in the case of Sam's family, and what we have focused on, is the deep distortion of their lives by the appalling evils they undergo: Sam's terrifying total paralysis as a child, his disruptive emotional and behavioral problems, his removal from his family and placement in residential schools for nine years, his mother's emotional illness, her suicide, and through it all the family's slow disintegration.

I have focused on this one concrete case because imagining redemption has to be correspondingly concrete. What redemption means in one case is not interchangeable with what it means in another case. Rather, Christianly speaking, what redemption means in one case is at most analogous to what it means in another. Redemption has to be imagined afresh in each case.

Furthermore, from a Christian perspective, redemption may mean more than one thing in any one case. For example, in chapter 2 we explored the redemptive difference Jesus can make for Sam's family when the word *redeem* means "make up for" a bad performance or event, while in chapter 3 we explored the redemptive difference Jesus can make for the same situation when *redeem* means "to redeem from," to regain someone or something that has been alienated.

PUBLIC AND PRIVATE REDEMPTION

Liberation and political theologies have criticized traditional and modern Christian accounts of redemption for ignoring or under-emphasizing the public and social character of God's redemptive work in and through Jesus. Imagining redemption as making up for a bad performance or regaining what was alienated are at risk of similar rebuke from these theologies, which represent the most important theological movement of the past half century. If I were to argue that these two senses of redemption exhausted the meanings of redemption, then this book's account of redemption, too, would be subject to the same critique.

However, redemption can also be imagined as the fulfilling of a promise, and this third understanding is not subject to the objections of liberation theologies. Redemption as "fulfilling a promise" is systematically interrelated with redemption as "making up for" the world's bad performance and as "redemption from" bondage to distorted personal identities; each of the three can be fully imagined only when it is imagined in relation to the other two. It is this third way of imagining, however, that keeps this interrelated complex of ways of imagining redemption from being just one more account open to criticism by liberation and political theologies.

Before any further discussion, we must first clarify what liberation and political theologies object to in most traditional and modern accounts of redemption. That, in turn, will call for clarification of just what it is about human persons that is changed when God relates to them redemptively. In other words, what is it about human beings that makes them vulnerable to falling into a predicament that requires redemption? And what is it about them that is susceptible to the difference that God's redemptive relating can make?

The objection that a theological idea is inadequate must have a basis; that is, some standard of "adequacy" must be identified. In this case the standard is easily identified; it is the New Testament writers' witness to God's redemptive relating to humankind in Jesus of Nazareth in order to redeem the evil humankind undergoes. More exactly, the critique rests on a feature of that witness that New Testament scholarship has stressed is absolutely central to it, although it is counterintuitive to us: New Testament writers imagine God's redemptive relating as the beginning of the *eschaton*, the inauguration of the end time that brings both a final disclosure of and a judgment on human estrangement from God, as well as the blessing of God's just rule in a new creation.

The New Testament writers imagined this eschatological, divine redemptive relating as something public and exterior to us, not purely private and interior. Paul, for example, imagines redemption as a "new creation." The Apocalypse of John pictures it culminating in a "new heaven and earth," a new cosmos. A new creation, a new cosmos is a new, observable public world "outside" us.

The critique of familiar accounts of redemption stresses above all that because they imagine redemption largely as an issue of human interiority, they are inadequate to the redemption to which the New Testament witnesses. Although the primary critique is that traditional and modern accounts make redemption look extremely individualistic, the nub of the matter, I think, is that they lead to imagining God's redemptive work as largely *interior* and private, so that redemption, in turn, is seen chiefly as a change in the human heart or consciousness.

According to its critics, imagining redemption in such an interiorized way raises several questions: How are redemptive changes of people's "insides" related to their "outsides," to the public world in which they live and its arrangements of all sorts of powers? How are redemptive changes of their "interiorities" related to redeemed persons' publicly observable behavior in that external world? Generalized, the question is this: How are the private and the public aspects of human beings related to each other? Liberationist and political theologians rightly point out that it is difficult to see how there can be any *necessary* connection between an interior change and a subsequent change in our exterior, observable, public world; its arrangements of power; and our bodily practices in that world. If the important difference redemption makes to people is to change their private "interiority," then it seems a secondary and optional matter whether that change also involves changes in their public "exteriority." But, the critique goes, a focus on redemption as a change in interior human subjectivity, which makes redemption seem inherently private, sits poorly with New Testament imagining of redemption as bringing not only new subjectivities but also a new creation.

IN WHAT DOES REDEMPTION MAKE A DIFFERENCE?

This critique of privatizing redemption also brings out the point that imagining redemption is systematically inseparable from imagining human being. Every understanding of redemption assumes the validity of some account of what it is to be a human person who is, first, capable of getting into a predicament that requires redemption and, second, capable of undergoing redemptive change. The presupposed account of what it is to be human determines, in turn, just what it is about us that is imagined to be changed by God's redemptive relating to us in Jesus.

In traditional accounts, God's redemptive relating makes a difference initially and chiefly in people's souls as opposed to their bodies. Living human bodies, so this reasoning goes, because they are made of matter, can be perceived by the senses. Further, because they are made of three-dimensional matter that is organized in a highly ordered way, they require a three-dimensional material context or cosmos that is also structured in an orderly way and is shared with other material bodies. Thus, human bodies are observable and share and act in public space. What gives life to a living human body, however, is distinguishable from the body itself. The evidence for this is that when a living body dies, although the body remains in its three-dimensional materiality, its life is gone. What gives life to a human body is called its soul. The soul is "spiritual" not "material." That is, it is not made of matter, is not perceptible, and does not have dimensions. It is the interior, not exterior, of human beings.

It is only fair to stress that in this traditional way of imagining what it is that makes human beings human, being human is not identified with being a soul and human beings are not usually imagined as radically individual atoms. A human being is neither a soul nor a body alone, but the composite of the two in a *living* human body. Furthermore, human beings are inherently social creatures. Thus our relationships with other human beings are essential to us and not just accidental modifications of us. Our distortion as creatures fallen in sin lies in our solidarity with one another "in" fallen Adam; our redeemed reality lies in our solidarity with one another "in" Christ. Premodern Christian thinkers shared the view that the "in" consists of a relationship to others that constitutes both what we are as humans and who we each are individually.

All the same, it is specifically the soul that makes it possible for a person to fall into a predicament that requires redemption, and it is in the soul that God's active relating to such a person can make a redemptive difference. As they are traditionally imagined, human souls are created by God and have the powers of intellect and free will. Since one wills what one desires, and desiring is the root of loving, and the symbolic seat of love is the heart, the "will" is often symbolized by *heart*. Because the soul includes both intellect and will, "head" and "heart," it is possible for the soul to go wrong, to love the wrong things, to guide the body into actions that rationally aim to achieve the wrong goals in so habituated a way that the whole human being falls into bondage to sin. It is the soul that makes a human person capable of getting into a predicament that requires redemption.

It follows then that redemption must be understood as a change chiefly in a person's soul that turns it to love its true good—God. But that is to say that when God relates in Jesus to human persons to redeem the evil they undergo, the redemptive difference occurs primarily and chiefly in their "hearts and minds," in their interiority, and not in the exterior public world that they share and is their embracing context.

In contrast, in typically modern accounts God's redemptive relating makes a difference initially and chiefly in human persons' consciousness or subjectivity as opposed to their physical, social, and cultural "givenness." Here the core contrast is between the "determinateness" of the givens of a human being and a human being's "freedom," rather than between the matter of a living human body ("body") and the life of a living human body ("soul").

With respect to its social, cultural, and physical "givens," including its neurological and hormonal givens, a human being is as determined as is the movement of any piece of machinery. At least in principle, in respect to its "givens" a human being is as appropriate a subject for rigorous investigation by the physical and social sciences and as subject to measurement, analysis, manipulation, and control as any other subject of scientific study. In this regard, human being is "objective." Its "givens" are its "objectivity."

In another respect, however, human beings exhibit freedom from their "givens." Here "freedom" is understood less as "freedom of choice among alternatives" than as the capacity for self-transcendence, that is, the capacity to stand back from oneself or stand out from oneself *as given*. The very fact that human beings are conscious that they are in many respects "given" shows that they have the capacity to distance themselves from those "givens."

In this view, human freedom is not the absence of determined and constraining "givens," but (1) the capacity to know that those givens are there, (2) the capacity to imagine them to be different, and (3) above all, the capacity to decide what attitude one will adopt toward them. In this regard, human being is "subjective." Its self-transcending consciousness is its "subjectivity," and it systematically eludes all efforts to measure, analyze, manipulate, and control it.

The importance of distinguishing between human objectivity and human subjectivity is twofold: (1) only subjects are morally accountable beings, and (2) only other subjects lay moral obligations and duties on us. Subjects lay a claim on us to respect them as good in themselves and not just as objects that may be good for some use. They impose on us the moral duty always to treat them as ends and never as means. Objects, on the other hand, lay no moral duties on us. They are not ends in themselves and may be used, within the limits of prudence, as means and instruments.

It is only fair to note that in this modern way of imagining what it is that makes human beings human, being human is not identified with being a "subject" in any simple way and human beings are not imagined as radically individual atoms. Human being is imagined not as a composite but as an ongoing, living dialectic between "objectivity" and "subjectivity." Further, this way of imagining human being tends to stress the idea that self-transcending consciousness is inherently an "intersubjectivity." Subjects are inherently social realities. This theme is especially important in the work of Christian "existentialists." For example, although his existentialism is often characterized as promoting a profoundly individualistic view of human nature, Søren Kierkegaard is clear in *Works of Love*[1] that relationships are constitutive of human subjects. And in his discussion of Christian existence, Rudolf Bultmann[2] is explicit that human existence is constituted by intersubjective relationships.

All the same, it is specifically human subjectivity that makes it possible for a human person to fall into a predicament that requires redemption, and it is in human subjectivity that God's active relating to such a person is imagined as making a redemptive difference. Preserving one's capacity for self-transcending consciousness or subjectivity is not itself a given. It is a lifelong project to be a "subject." Ironically, preserving one's subjectivity depends on how one relates to oneself and how one exercises self-transcending consciousness in the way one situates oneself in the world. If the way you, so to speak, deploy yourself in the world fails to mark the distinction between your subjectivity and objectivity, you will end up simply identifying yourself with your "givenness" or objectivity. You will live as though you were nothing other than what your society, culture, and physical heritage determined you to be, and you will be an interchangeable replica of everyone else who is determined by the same society and its culture, uncritically following its conventional behaviors, thinking its received wisdom and clichés, aspiring to realize its stock values and tastes. You will be an individual, but you will not be a subject because you will have "objectified" yourself, surrendering the capacity for self-transcendence and remaining in bondage to "objectivity." Objectified yourself, you will be inclined to relate to other human beings as useful "objects" to be analyzed, manipulated, and controlled for your own purposes rather than as "subjects" who, in their freedom, ought not be manipulated as means to one's own ends but ought rather to be treated as moral ends in their own rights. To live this way is to slip into a way of being in the world that requires redemption from objectification.

By the same token, redemption of a human person must be understood as a change chiefly in a person's subjectivity that restores consciousness's capacity for self-transcendence, thereby freeing it from its objectification. That is, when God relates in Jesus to human persons in order to redeem the evil they undergo, that relating makes a redemptive difference primarily and chiefly in the interiority of their subjectivities and not in the exterior public and "objective" world that they share as their embracing context.

According to liberation and political theologies, both traditional and modern imaginings of being human are inadequate to the New Testament writers' imagining of redemption because they either take the soul to be more basic than the body, or subjectivity than objectivity. They locate the difference redemption makes in the interiority of human persons' souls or subjectivities, that is, inside their "hearts and minds." Only secondarily does redemption make a difference in their exterior, public worlds. It is just assumed that if people's "hearts and minds" or "subjectivities" truly are changed, then their observable public behavior in shared social and cultural space, the ways in which they actually relate to their neighbors in everyday life, will change for the better. God's kingly rule will slowly be built as, one by one, people are changed.

However, the critique goes, when human beings are understood by positing that their private "interiorities" are more basic than their "exterior" lives in shared public space and time, it is difficult to see how changes in the former will lead to changes in the latter. Furthermore, there is little historical evidence that changes in people one by one lead to changes in the "powers and principalities" that structure their commonly shared public worlds. Yet it is inherent to God's redemption of evil to which New Testament writers witness that the difference made in the public realm is at least as fundamental as the difference made inside people's hearts and minds.

Christian accounts of redemption would seem generally to be systematically inseparable from accounts of being human. Liberationist and political theologies have argued persuasively that the inadequacy of traditional and modern ways of imagining redemption is a function of their reliance on positing a distinction between the private "interiority" of human beings and their public "exteriority." More adequate imagining of redemption must, at the very least, avoid depending on such a disjunction. The discussion that follows suggests a third way of imagining redemption that, when combined with the ways of imagining redemption explored in chapters 2 and 3, avoids relying on that disjunction.

PROMISES AND PUBLIC PERSONS

The sense of redemption as "redemption from" (chapter 3) is the more vulnerable of the ways of imagining redemption that we explored in chapters 2 and 3. "Redemption from" turns on what people trust to show that their lives are worth living. We considered Jesus' horrifying passion and death as God's concrete act of solidarity with the likes of Sam and his family precisely in the midst of their own horrific situations. So long as the family trusts that the respect that is accorded the sheer fact of their survival of terrible events proves their lives worthwhile, their personal identities will be defined by those events and will be fixed, closed in bondage to those past events. If, however, they trust that the worth of their lives is a function of God's freely loving them in a very concrete way as their fellow sufferer in Jesus' passion, then it is God's relating to them in love that defines their identities in ways that keep them open to the present and free from bondage to the past.

Jesus' presence can make that redemptive difference to Sam's family, but redemption turns on the question of what they trust to define who they are. Trust in God's love is certainly at the heart of faith in God. And trust in God is equally certainly a mode of subjectivity. Faith is human inwardness, as Kierkegaard has taught us, at its most intense. As such, it is interior. And thus redemption imagined mainly as "release from" bondage to an alien power appears to be open to the charge of being imagined in an interiorizing way.

In contrast, redemption imagined as making up for a bad performance is somewhat less open to the rebuke because of the features of promise making that we considered in chapter 2. For our discussion here we must draw those features out a bit more.

In chapter 2, redemption in the sense of "making up for" a bad performance or event turns, for Sam's family, on the relocation of their lives in a new embracing context. The immediate context that embraces their lives is a series of horrible situations that are anything but promising. In

Jesus' teaching and healing, God promises the imminent inbreaking of the long-expected new creation. God's act of promise making creates a new and promising context for Sam and his family that, in a way, "makes up for" the grievous losses they experienced.

When promise making, on one side, and living in trust of promises made, on the other, are understood simply as subjective acts, then this way of imagining redemption, too, is open to the charge of interiorizing redemption. However, promise making is more complex than that. Recall our discussion of what is involved in promise making. Informed by J. L. Austin's analysis of the "performative" force of many utterances, we noted several things about promises: Making a promise is not an "interior" act done in the privacy of one's own heart or consciousness and then reported or described or expressed outwardly in speech. Rather, it is a "performative" act of speech. As such, it is a public act that is governed by cultural conventions that specify, among other things, conditions under which the promise does or does not "misfire" and is or is not an "abuse" of the practice of promise making. Moreover, making a promise is a "commissive" speech act in which (1) the promiser binds him- or herself (not anyone else) (2) to a project (to bring about in future what has been promised) and (3) to a person or persons (to whom the promise is made), and then (4) invites them to self-involvingly commit themselves to the promiser in trust that he or she will indeed make good on the promise.

What needs to be stressed here is that the self-involving force of an act of a promise creates a new community—the community of the promiser and all those to whom the promise has been made. The act of promising and others' response of trust in the promiser binds these persons in a new society, whose size depends on the size of the group to whom the promise is made. A precondition for the creation of this new community is the existence of its larger host community, whose common language is used in making the promise and whose practices and social conventions are enacted in the act of promise making that created the new community and regulate it. This new community, like every human community, is itself organized by a particular arrangement of power, because the project of fulfilling a promise, which constitutes this new community, inherently involves human actions that are exercises of various types of power organized and ordered to particular ends. In short, this new community is, in a broad sense of the term, an institution, a new power structure.

In sum, making a promise is a public act that enacts a practice that is one part of the common life of a society and its culture. It results in a change in that society and its culture: the creation of a new community within it, an institution with its own distinctive structure of various sorts of power. The act of promise making and its consequences are part of the public realm.

Granted, this public realm is "socially constructed," and only conscious subjects are capable of social construction. There is no denying that human beings' subjectivities are necessary for promise making to take place. The point, however, is that those who make a promise and have subjective interiorities are first of all agents of public practices that constitute public spaces.

Those promise makers, by metaphorical extension, include God. So, imagining redemption for Sam's family as God's relocating their unpromising lives into a new promising context constituted by God's promise making is not necessarily an "interiorizing" way of imagining redemption.

Nonetheless, an account of the redemptive difference Jesus can make now for the situations that overcame Sam and his family will remain inadequate if it is imagined only in these two ways. Is there an additional way to imagine it Christianly that brings out more explicitly the public, exterior, objective dimension of the redemptive difference God can make in and through what Jesus does and undergoes?

REDEMPTION AS FULFILLING A PROMISE

A third way that we use expressions like "to redeem" and "redemption" in everyday English is in phrases like "redeeming a coupon," "redeeming a bond," or, in an earlier time, "redeeming" paper money for gold. Behind these examples is the picture implicit in our saying that someone "redeemed" a promise; that is, the promiser not only committed him- or herself to someone else by making that person a promise, but he or she made good on that promise, actually carried it out. So too, we may consider a coupon, a bond, and a piece of paper money to be implicit promises: if you submit that coupon, bond, or paper money to the proper person in the proper place, its implicit promise of a discount, or the return of initial investment, or gold, will be actualized. One sense of redemption in colloquial English, then, is "fulfilling a promise."

By metaphoric extension, Christians conventionally speak of God working in and through what Jesus does and undergoes not merely to make but to fulfill God's own promise to bring something new and good out of horrific events and horrendous situations in human life. We have noted that, in the narratives of the Synoptic Gospels, not only is it essential to Jesus' unsubstitutable personal identity that his proclamation simply *is* God promising the imminence of the end time, but that Jesus' personal presence is itself God making that promise. We explored in chapter 2 how this alone is one way that Jesus can make a redemptive difference here and now.

The Gospel narratives also make it essential to Jesus' personal identity that he is, in his own person, the inauguration of God's making good on that very promise. He is in his person God's beginning to fulfill the promise of eschatological blessing. The way the Synoptic Gospels tell it, God has only inaugurated the fulfillment of the eschatological promise; we await its full actualization. As the familiar theological slogan has it, the eschatological inbreaking is "now actual, but not yet fully actualized."

Despite their differences, Matthew's and Luke's narratives present Jesus' identity in the same way: they narrate Jesus' resurrection appearances to his disciples *as* the concrete inauguration of God's long-promised end time, in Galilee for Matthew and in Jerusalem for Luke. For Matthew (and Mark), Galilee's significance may have been that it was the site of Jesus' promise by word and healing of the imminent inbreaking of God's eschatological rule, a promise now made good in Jesus' resurrection. For Luke, Jerusalem's significance may have involved that city's central role in the history of Israel and its prophets' eschatological promises of divine redemption, now made good in the resurrection of Jesus, not just for Jesus' contemporaries but for all Israel. What Jesus does and undergoes in rising from the dead is God's concrete way of bringing a new creation out of the old; new life out of living deaths.

That leads us to the redemptive difference the risen Jesus can make for the situations Sam's family finds itself in and to imagine redemption in the sense of "fulfilling a promise."

VICIOUS CYCLES AND LIVING DEATHS

Human lives become living deaths when they endlessly rerun vicious cycles. The classic account of living vicious cycles is Hegel's analysis of the dynamics of the master-slave relationship in which each partner's life depends on the other's in such a way that each life is defined by the other. Relationships of dependence inherently involve an imbalance of power in some respects, but not in every respect. Slaves are dependent on their masters precisely, for example, because their masters have more of certain kinds of power than the slaves do. Hegel brilliantly recognized and explored, however, the fact that masters become similarly dependent on their slaves because the slaves have certain kinds of power the masters need but lack. The life of each is thus reciprocally defined by the other.

This holds true in all lives lived out in relations marked by dependency and imbalances of power: relations of parents and children, employers and employees, leaders and followers, teachers and students, friends, and lovers. The fact that some of these relationships are voluntary rather than coerced, warm rather than cold, personal and informal rather than impersonal and formal, makes no difference to the fact of power imbalance in the relationship. A relation of dependence means a relation with power imbalance. But that is not what makes such relationships *vicious* cycles.

Relationships in which each partner depends on the other in such a way that each one's life is defined by the other become vicious cycles when the relationship diminishes either or both partners. The variations on this are boundless. Human beings are endlessly imaginative in devising ways to diminish those who are in some respect or other dependent on them. Usually such diminishment involves excluding those who are dependent—from community of mutual esteem with those on whom they depend; from participating in making major decisions about their own lives; from various sorts of social, political, and economic power; or, in its most radical form, from the circle of the "truly human."

In its endless varieties, the act of excluding that diminishes dependent others seems to be inescapable. As Miroslav Volf has pointed out, the separation from the other that is necessary to constitute and maintain the dynamic of one's own life in relation to the other "slides into exclusion that seeks to affirm" one's life "at the expense of the other. The power of sin from without—the system of exclusion—thrives on both the power and the powerlessness from within, the irresistible power of the will to be oneself and the powerlessness to resist the slippage into exclusion of the other."[3] All acts of exclusion have one thing in common: they express a fundamental attitude of contempt for the dependent ones, no matter how unconscious, subtle, even genial the contempt may be.

Exclusion, and the contempt it expresses, diminishes the partners in any relationships who are in some respect dependent on the other partners. These dependent partners, in turn, respond to their exclusion with resentment and retaliation. Inasmuch as those they depend on in some respects are dependent on them in other respects, exclusion and diminishment are also reciprocated. Further, since human beings are inherently interdependent beings, when we diminish the life of another who depends on us in some way, we diminish the life of one on whom we depend in other ways, so that we diminish our own life at the same time. This cycle of mutual diminishment is self-perpetuating and has no built-in ending. Diminishment of another's life and of one's own violates both other and self.

In a broad sense every diminishment of our partners' lives in relationships in which they are in some respect dependent on us is in one way or another an act of violence against them and, by the same token, against our own life. We oppress both them and ourselves, and we generate a vicious cycle of violence and oppression. The cycle spirals endlessly into new forms of reciprocal exclusion, diminishment, violation, and oppression.

When life is lived as an endless cycle of mutual exclusion, diminishment, and oppression, it is a living death. The pattern is familiar enough. It has, in fact, provided a fundamental mythic structure for modern theater since Ibsen, although it was recognized well before the modern world. As Rowan Williams points out in his extraordinary book on the resurrection of Jesus,

> We are born into a world where there is *already* a history of oppression and victimization. . . . And so, before we can be conscious of it, the system of oppressor-victim relations absorbs

us. It is this 'already' which theology . . . refers to as original sin—the sense of a primordial 'diminution' from which we all suffer before ever we are capable of understanding or choice.[4]

The basic pattern of a living death is familiar enough in the abstract; but you can live it for years without recognizing what you are doing.

When life is this living death, the distortion of personal identity that we discussed in chapter 3 is not what needs redeeming. What needs redeeming here is the distorting *pattern* of the flow of our life as day by day we interrelate with others, not the distorted way we define the "who" that each of us takes into a relationship. This pattern in human relations that turns God's gift of life into a living death was well established before we appeared on the scene. We are born into it. The question facing us is what might be meant by the "redemption" of such living death.

In their relationship Sam and his father lived their own version of vicious cycles. Both of them were deeply dependent, albeit in different ways, on two immensely powerful, supraindividual powers: the system comprising teaching and research hospitals that had saved Sam's life in the first place and to which they returned for help with every new medical crisis; and the state Department of Children and Youth Services that managed Sam's school placements and social work support system after he was declared permanently disabled, placed on Disability Social Security, and declared eligible for federal assistance through Title 19. Sam was totally dependent on his father to access the appropriate medical and social service assistance, to negotiate the intricate and slow bureaucracy of each system, to keep track of records, to make and keep appointments, and to sustain communication with Sam's caseworkers to ensure that he did not fall between the cracks.

Those two systems structured the public world Sam and his father lived in. They were among its powers and principalities. Sam had no comprehension of how the system worked, and even after several years of practice, his father doubted that he did either. He could claim no countervailing power to exercise in self-protection against these systems. In fact, the systems exercised something close to absolute power, on which Sam and his father were almost absolutely dependent. The phrase "absolute dependence" has particularly appropriate resonances for this discussion, for Friedrich Schleiermacher[5] uses it to describe the feeling that for him is the basis of religious experience; Sam and his father experienced the medical care and social service systems in something close to a demonically distorted version of "religious" experience. In their interactions with these two systems Sam and his father were virtually nonpersons. They were excluded from the processes that made major decisions about Sam's treatment and care. On one hand, Sam's father genuinely liked the individual representatives of these two systems with whom they dealt, pitifully overworked folk who were unfailingly nice and well-meaning. He could not help but be grateful that what they provided made a life possible for Sam and himself. On the other hand, sheer helpless dependence generated a mixture of compliant passivity, terror that Sam might not respond to medical treatment or that the state agency might drop him, and unacknowledged rage. He needed a clients' liberation movement, but at the time he was incapable of imagining, much less founding such a thing.

Between them Sam and his father lived a vicious cycle. At his residential school Sam responded to his classmates' exclusion of him, to his feelings of guilt over his mother's death, and to missing his family, by acting out to get attention. This behavior subjected him to more intense behavior modification procedures, which simply confirmed his picture that he was a bad person. It also distracted him from school work, which his short-term memory problems made difficult enough. His poor academic performance confirmed his conviction that he was inferior to his classmates. He depended almost entirely on his father for assurance that in fact he belonged to a family who loved him and that he was not guilty of his mother's death. At the same time, Sam's anger that he was not permitted to live at home was aimed at his father, whom he simultaneously feared might punish him in some even more dreadful way.

Concurrently, his father grieved Sam as the son he had lost—the son who had once been full of promise; who would finish college, find a satisfying career, be a self-sufficient and contributing member of society; the son who would perhaps marry and have children; who would become his adult friend; the son who had been replaced by this damaged adolescent-infant who would, it seemed, never grow up. Sam's deep dependence on him, both emotional and financial, terrified him because it seemed unlikely ever to end and therefore promised to bankrupt him in every way. Unsurprisingly, his father related to Sam in infantilizing ways, hovering protectively over Sam emotionally while at the same time remaining emotionally self-protective and distant from him.

So the two played into the living death of this very specific spiraling cycle. The father's infantilizing solicitude encouraged Sam's emotional dependence on him, which only heightened the father's anxiety about the future while it undercut the school's efforts to help Sam acquire a measure of self-reliance, thus giving Sam new reasons to feel like a failure. That, in turn, fed the father's grief over the Sam he had lost. Sam, in turn, interpreted his father's grief as deep disappointment in him, which reinforced his already intense guilt and his acting out. Sam's failure to make progress in either the school's academic program or its behavioral modification program intensified his father's grief at how much he had lost in Sam and his anxiety about Sam's future and what that meant about his own future.

BREAKING VICIOUS CYCLES

So we again ask, what earthly difference could the crucified and risen Jesus make here?

The apostle Paul, writing our earliest witness to Jesus' resurrection appearances, sees the resurrection as the event in which God begins to make good on the promise that God's end-time rule will break in. Jesus' resurrection is the "firstfruits" (1 Cor. 15:20, 23; cf. Rom. 8:23) of the end time, the inauguration, though not the full actualization, of the eschatological new creation. It promises to break the vicious cycles of life, like the cycle between Sam and his father that patterned their lives. It promises to break the vicious cycles lived out in a world deformed in the image of what we have come to call original sin. It promises new life out of living death.

Matthew and John narrate appearances by the crucified Jesus to his disciples in ways that suggest how the risen Jesus can make a redemptive difference for the likes of Sam and his father. In contrast to Luke, Matthew and John locate in quite different ways Jesus' resurrection appearances in Galilee rather than in Jerusalem. The disciples are told to go there and Jesus would meet them.

Galilee is where the pattern of the disciples' lives and interrelationships had been formed before they met Jesus. It is into their old creation that they are sent, where they once were fishermen; where they began to follow Jesus; where uncomprehending, they misunderstood him; where, distrusting, they feared for him and for themselves. When he does appear to them there following his crucifixion, he re-forms their lives anew by giving them a vocation: In Matthew, "Go and make disciples of all nations" (28:19a); in John, specifically to Peter, three times, "Feed my lambs" (21:15b, 16b, 17b) and twice, "Follow me" (21:19, 22).

However, the basic pattern of this new life is ambiguous. The fact that it is *in Galilee* that their lives are patterned anew in relation to Jesus reminds us that they had returned to their earlier lives, the lives they had had before Jesus ever came along. John is explicit: they were fishermen again. The fact that they are in Galilee also reminds us that although for a while their interrelationships had been formed by their relation to Jesus as his followers, that pattern of life had dissolved when he was apprehended, tried, and crucified. And their being in Galilee reminds us, finally, of their failure: their cowardice and betrayal of Jesus.

Perhaps Jesus' crucifixion seemed to them to have invalidated his proclamation; surely it also drew their lives into a vicious cycle of guilt, shame, self-accusation, perhaps mutual recrimination. Do we not get a glimpse of that cycle at the end of John's narrative? In John 21 the disciples have returned as instructed to the shores of the Sea of Tiberias (or the Sea of Galilee). Under the leadership of Peter, who at Jesus' trial had denied knowing him, they fish all night and catch nothing. Just after daybreak someone appears on the beach and tells them to cast their nets on the right side of the boat. They make a large catch. The author makes a point of telling us that it is the disciple who is called the "beloved," not Peter (who is by implication not "beloved"), who then recognizes the man as Jesus. The disciples come ashore. Apparently Peter alone does the heavy lifting, hauling their catch out of the boat. Fish are cooking, and Jesus invites them to breakfast.

Then there is a reconciliation scene between Peter and Jesus. Three times Peter is given the opportunity to affirm his love for Jesus. He is the only one asked to do so, as if, given his denial of Jesus, *his* love alone were in question. This sharply contrasts Peter with the disciple consistently described as "beloved," who is usually identified as John. Three times Jesus gives Peter a special role to "feed" or "tend" his sheep, singling him out for a role no other disciple is assigned. Perhaps this new vocation signals his reconciliation with Jesus. Jesus then indicates "the kind of death by which he [Peter] would glorify

God" (21:19), whereupon the author pointedly has Peter ask Jesus about the "beloved" disciple and what would happen to him. And Jesus reportedly tells him, in effect, to mind his own business: ". . . what is that to you?" (21:23). Yes, the one who denies his Lord is once again reconciled with his Lord and is still recognized as the disciples' leader. But the text suggests that there remains a good bit of rivalry and perhaps even mutual suspicion between Peter and John, who did not deny the Lord and who is the truly "beloved" one. What else does this competition between the two signify if not that in their own way their lives have been caught in some version of a vicious cycle?

And yet in Galilee Jesus accepts them just as they are in their complicated lives, accepts them as fishermen who once had begun to live as fishers-of-persons, accepts them as faithless fishers-of-persons, and calls them to a new life. That call breaks the vicious cycles that have shaped their relationships since the scene in the garden of Gethsemane and at the trial. God's forgiving call in the risen Jesus means new life in the midst of the vicious cycles of their living deaths.

It would take them the rest of their lives to live into that vocation, to learn to live as forgiven persons.

SANCTIFICATION: IT'S FREE BUT IT'S NOT CHEAP

It is a lifelong process to live into God's new creation, the traditional name for which is sanctification. The living has been long and slow for Sam and his father. The new creation surfaces only fragmentarily in odd moments in their lives. When he turned twenty-one, past the age when he could be covered by mandate of the state's Department of Children and Youth Services, and when he would have to leave residential school, Sam earned his General Education Diploma, his high school equivalency certificate. He could not have been prouder had he earned a PhD. Rightly so. It had been a hard road, and for Sam it was and remains a sign that he could learn and grow. He relocated nearer his father and became part of a publicly funded program that provides a well-organized social and medical support system. He is able to live on his own in a small, rent-subsidized apartment. For Sam all this is a sign that he can be self-reliant and can live independent of his father.

For his part, Sam's father slowly has lived into seeing and loving Sam for the person he is now and not as the reminder of a son he lost. He has begun to delight in Sam's thoughtfulness, his intense if fleeting empathy for other people's sorrows and joys, his sense of humor, his sweet spirit. Years after Sam left residential school his father began to meet younger parents whose children were afflicted with quite different and profoundly serious illnesses, and who were totally dependent on the medical and social service systems but were far less passive than Sam's father had been. These parents figured out ways to challenge the edicts of the medical and social service systems when that seemed necessary. Sam's father went through a process of consciousness raising. He began to see how a clients' liberation movement was entirely possible.

Sam and his father have each been living into a life that is not formed in a vicious cycle of interaction with the other's life. It is a slow process, nothing dramatic, not very consistent, never a straight line, down as often as up. Nevertheless, by God's grace, it is a process of real change. It had to be by God's gracious working within them because neither is up to it on his own.

The grace of new creation breaking into the old and breaking open the vicious cycles that made the old a living death is unconditional. God has begun to make good on the promise God freely gave in the ministry of Jesus but has not yet fully actualized that promise. Similarly, God's redemption of the situation that overcame Sam and his family is not yet fully realized. Like all of us, they live in the mean time, the between time after Easter and before the general resurrection.

In that time the grace of the new creation is free. But it is not cheap. As Galilee signifies for the disciples their failure and betrayal precisely when they are being given new lives, so living into the new creation has meant for Sam and his father the pain of honest confrontation and the acknowledgment of their failures of each other, their rage at each other, their fear and distrust of each other. In the resurrection of the crucified Jesus God inaugurates a new creation, but we live into it only by passing through full disclosure and judgment of who we are. Not only is the end time, inaugurated in the resurrection of Jesus, the time of a new creation, it is also the final judgment day. The God who comes among us redemptively is also the righteous One before whom each is revealed and known for who she is, for who he is.

That is why the word of God to Sam and his family, and to every horrendous situation people may find themselves in, lies in the apostle's words to the Philippians to live in fear and trembling, for the One with whom they have to do is God:

> Work out your own salvation with fear and trembling; for it is God who is at work in you, enabling you both to will and to work for his good pleasure.
>
> (Phil. 2:12b, 13)

Coda

In his church's Sunday morning adult education hour my friend Milton asked for someone to explain what "redemption" means. After all, he said, the word is "all over" the texts Christians read in church; the things Christians say in church; and the practices of prayer, praise, education, and pastoral care that make up the common life of Christian communities. But, he reported, no one said anything. At the time I didn't know whether to laugh or groan. I've come to believe, however, that in a way silence may have been the best response. Or perhaps "It all depends." For while "redemption" has several meanings, Christianly speaking it does not mean any one thing that can be neatly summarized in a general way. In chapters 2, 3, and 4 I have urged that what "redemption" means Christianly speaking depends on the concrete particulars of actual situations in which people undergo horrendous evil that cry out for redemption. Moreover, the redemption of any one such situation may mean more than one thing.

These chapters have been about what "redemption" means "Christianly speaking." Their form has to be consistent with their thesis. That is, rather than offer an abstract "doctrine of redemption" that purports to comprehend what redemption means in any and all cases regardless of their particularities, these chapters needed to be written in a form that conveys the concreteness of both what needs redemption and of its actual redemption. So in them I have imagined not redemption in general but the redemption of one particular sequence of horrific situations that happened to a boy called Sam and his family. However, that entire approach raises at least three problems.

First, this approach runs the danger that the emotionally upsetting power of a particularly horrendous situation will divert our attention from imagining God's redemption of those situations to the human drama of the situations themselves. This book is not about Sam and his family. It is about redemption as Christians imaginatively understand it. It will have failed in its purpose if it proves to be more engaging about Sam and his family than illuminating about redemption.

Second, what these chapters urge *Christianly speaking* about redemption from bondage to distorted personal identities and about redemption as the breaking of vicious cycles in people's lives will quite rightly be said to sound a great deal like things said in nontheological ways about the dynamics of *psychological* "healing" of distortions of self-identity and of vicious interpersonal cycles. The challenge "How are they different?" naturally arises. Aren't the theological meanings of redemption just alternative ways of making the same point that psychological analyses make, albeit perhaps less rigorously?

Third, these chapters regularly speak of "imagining" redemption. If that does not mean that redemption is something imagined, that is, largely imaginary as opposed to real, then doesn't it confirm the objection in the second problem? Doesn't it amount to saying that Christian talk of redemption is an imaginatively elaborated, fantasized version of familiar psychological dynamics?

My task now is to address these three problems. The discussion will not add anything to our efforts in earlier chapters to imagine redemption. There is no end to the task so long as there are new situations in need of redemption. However, since the unexamined writing isn't worth reading, I will reflect on some aspects of how theological explication of redemption is best done.

SYSTEMATICALLY UNSYSTEMATIC THEOLOGY

The effort to ward off the danger that these chapters will be read as a book about Sam and his family rather than as a book about redemption dictates a major feature of the book's structure. The book combines aspects of two types of theology that are usually kept distinct: systematic theology and pastoral theology.

What are they? First, what makes both of them "theology" is that they are ways of engaging in the enterprise St. Anselm of Canterbury called "faith seeking understanding." Pastoral theology, broadly speaking, seeks to throw light on the theological content, rationale, and criteria of truly faithful Christian ministry. Sometimes the term *pastoral theology* is used in a way that seems to equate it simply with pastoral counseling. Historically,[1] however, it has been used much more broadly to mean critical reflection on the entire range of practices that make up both the common life of communities of Christian faith and the lives of individual persons of faith. These practices include prayer, worship, preaching, education, moral guidance, healing, support in times of crisis, hospitality, and friendship;[2] they are ways that members of communities of Christian faith serve one another and their neighbors who are not members of the community.

Also speaking broadly, systematic theology seeks to throw light on the meaning and truth of beliefs that are inseparable from the practices that make up the life of communities and persons of Christian faith. Because there are different ways in which such an enterprise may be done "systematically," there are at least three different ways it may be "systematic."

At the very least, systematic theology is systematic in the way it proceeds, starting with what are taken to be the simplest and most easily understood beliefs and moving step by step to explain more and more complex and difficult ideas about God and all other realities as God relates to them and they relate to God.

Second, it may be systematic in its effort to show how Christian beliefs about these matters are systematically interconnected, pointing out how they sometimes regularly follow one from another, sometimes are regularly in tension with one another, sometimes regularly constrain one another, sometimes regularly enrich and complexify one another. That is, systematic theology may show that the relations among Christian beliefs are ruled by something like a grammar.

Third, it may be systematic in that it proposes a coherent scheme of more or less rigorously defined technical concepts by which Christian beliefs can be reformulated to provide an internally coherent network of explanations that are adequate to all aspects of human experience. Usually such a scheme of concepts is borrowed from some work of systematic philosophy so that theology in this style is called philosophical theology. This book is "systematic" in the first two ways. It tries to move from thought to thought in a systematic way, and it traces out systematic connections between Christian beliefs about redemption and a number of other Christian beliefs. However, it does not set out to be systematic in the third way. It does not promote a systematic structure of technical philosophical doctrine as the intellectual framework that will explain the meaning of Christian beliefs most profoundly or demonstrate their truth most persuasively.

For all of the vagueness about what kinds of enterprises pastoral theology and systematic theology are, the distinction between them has come to seem self-evident and to be taken for granted. One way this assumption manifests itself is in the expectations of the writing style appropriate to each. Works of systematic theology are expected to be both formally structured and conceptually abstract, as befits the construction of theory. Works of pastoral theology are expected to be concrete, even anecdotal, and although certainly not devoid of abstract conceptual "tools," they are expected to be less architectonic and more narrative in form.

Furthermore, it is tacitly assumed, at least in North America, that systematic theology is related to pastoral theology as theorizing is related to application of theory. Perhaps this is not surprising in a culture that is so heavily shaped by economic dependence on the transition from pure scientific research to the manufacture of consumer products. So, the tacit picture has it, systematic theologians "theorize" the intellectual context of Christian faith, and pastoral theologians look for ways in which some of that theory, combined with theory drawn from the psychological and social sciences, can be applied to help solve problems in the lives of persons and communities of faith. Creative "model" programs or techniques are developed out of such application, and the successful ones are promoted by denominational agencies, publishers, and entrepreneurial clergy.

This book is a systematic effort to subvert this theory-application picture of how systematic and pastoral theology are both distinguished from one another and related to one another. Rather than elaborate yet another theory about the true nature of systematic theology and pastoral theology, it has seemed to me that the best way to subvert that picture is to attempt to think theologically in a different way about some commonly recognized theological topic—such as redemption. So in reflecting theologically on redemption in this book I interweave questions, ways of thinking, and ways of writing that are conventionally confined either to systematic or to pastoral theology. If the doing is effective, its "method" will have been justified. If the doing is ineffective, it will not have mattered how persuasive the arguments are on behalf of the method. However, some explanation is in order and can be briefly given.[3]

The analogy "systematic theology is to pastoral theology as theory is to application of theory" is false. The nub of the matter, I think, lies in the fact that not every Christian belief can be "theorized." Consequently, *systematic theology* cannot be defined as "that inquiry that theorizes Christian beliefs (theories which may then be applied in pastoral theology)." Correlatively, *pastoral theology* should not be defined as "that inquiry that applies theological theories (formulated by systematic theology) to concrete cases in the lives of persons and communities of Christian faith."

"Theorize" is a slippery idea, for there is no one standard concept of theory. However, the distinctions I wish to draw require only a loose and informal notion of theory according to which a theory proposes a set of general principles that can explain an event or situation of which there may, in principle, be an indefinite number of others of the same type. In any given case, of course, there may not actually be any other instances of the event or situation being explained. For example, there may be only one wingless bird left in the world, but evolutionary theory needs to be able to explain it no less than it would need to explain a population of millions of wingless birds. Theories in the natural and social sciences tend to be like this.

In this regard, however, the beliefs that Christian systematic theology explicates are not all of one type. Some beliefs can be explicated as theories; some cannot. Some are more complex, and, straddling the distinction, they can be explicated as theories in certain respects and not in other respects.

In the first group are many beliefs about how God is related to a great many situations or events, so that there are many instances to which the beliefs refer. Indeed, in some cases they are beliefs about how God is related in the same way to *all* situations and events. Thus, traditional beliefs about God's omnipresence, omniscience, and omnipotence hold that God is present to, has knowledge of, and exercises power in relation universally to each and every situation and event. Traditional Christian beliefs about God's sustaining creation, continuing creation, and general providence are similar in this regard. Theological beliefs of this sort are clearly open to being theorized in the sense of "theory" invoked here. It is appropriate that when they are explicated as theories they are framed in rigorously structured, conceptually abstract ways. Thus, for example, belief in God's providence can be explicated in terms of a metaphysical theory of causality that can give a metaphysical explanation of every causal event whatever, including God's providential governance of the world.

A second group of beliefs contains Christian beliefs about absolutely unique situations or events that *in principle* cannot have more than one instance. The traditional belief that God created from nothing *all* reality of whatever sort other than God is such a belief. So too is the traditional belief about the incarnation in this world of the Second Person of the Trinity, and the belief that by his crucifixion he atoned "once and for all" for human sin. So too is the belief that God's actualization of the eschatological kingdom will bring a new creation. The appropriate form of theological explication of Christian beliefs of this type, I think, is not to "theorize" them but to offer remarks about the form and dynamics of the normative or canonical narratives in which these singular events are usually rendered in Christian discourse.

If the beliefs explicated by systematic theology include beliefs of both of these types, then *systematic theology* cannot be defined as the enterprise of developing a single, rigorous, systematic, internally coherent, comprehensive body of "theory" of Christian faith. Nor can it be kept sharply distinct from another theological discipline called *pastoral theology* on the supposition that while pastoral theology's task is to figure out how to "apply" the theory to problems that arise in Christian practice, systematic theology's effort to formulate the theory must be kept "pure" (as in "pure theory"), that is, separate from and prior to all concerns with Christian practice. On the contrary, in regard to at least some Christian beliefs, the line between systematic and pastoral theology rightly blurs. Correlatively, while it is appropriate that the form of thought and writing for systematic theological explication of some Christian beliefs be rigorously structured and conceptually abstract, it is equally appropriate that in explicating other types of Christian beliefs it be closely tied to the concrete particularities of the form and dynamics of normative Christian narratives.

Christian beliefs about redemption, with some of which this book has concerned itself, belong to a third group. Some beliefs about redemption can be theorized in certain respects; in other respects they cannot. For example, insofar as redemption is *God's* once-and-for-all act of atonement of the sin human persons do it is in principle utterly unique. By definition, it is a class of one. A major part of theologian Colin Gunton's legacy is his provocative argument in *The Actuality of Atonement*[4] that the more closely God's act of atonement is identified with God's unique act of incarnation, the clearer it is that atonement cannot be theorized and must instead be explicated by comment on the structure and dynamics of the canonical narratives that render Jesus' unsubstitutable personal identity. However, when atonement is considered with respect not to God's act but to changes in the way human beings' lives are "justified" and made holy by grace, then something like a theory is possible, for it is not a singular event. There are multiple instances of persons being "justified" and "sanctified."

So too, to invoke the distinction I have relied on in this book, insofar as redemption is not God's act of atonement of the evil people *do* but the promise and actualization of God's eschatological re-creation of horrific consequences of the evil they *undergo*, it is a "singularity." The appropriate mode of discourse for systematic theological explication of redemption is not "theory" but remarks about the way the narratives work that render that promise and its actualization, and remarks about what their broader implications might be.

At the same time, when eschatological re-creation is considered with respect not to God's performative act of promising and actualizing the promise but with respect to changes in persons' lives, then in one way something like theory seems possible. There are multiple instances of human lives overtaken by horrendous evil that God redeems. So the appropriate mode of discourse for systematic theology would be abstractly conceptual and as rigorously structured as possible. Historically, the result of such "theorizing" of redemption as eschatological re-creation has been relentlessly formal, highly general, and, finally, not very illuminating of the practices of Christian life, both individual and communal, that it was supposed to illumine.

In another way, though, the very effort to theorize such redemption is highly problematic. Each of the multiple instances is specific to the particularities and concrete situations of the persons involved. Just what "redemption" means, I have argued, is relative to those particularities. Each case is something like a "singularity." The sort of discourse each case calls for precisely in a *systematic* theological explication of meanings of redemption is a set of remarks on the structure and dynamics of a concretely particular narrative. The narrative functions not as illustrative or decoratively anecdotal but precisely as one major way in which the theological explication is done.

One major way; but not the only way. The mixed character of redemption as a theological topic, "singular" in some respects and not in others, calls for the style of theological explication employed in chapters 2, 3, and 4. It calls for theology that is *systematically unsystematic*. That is, it requires a style of theological explication of redemption that weaves together (1) systematic remarks about a narrative of a situation in need of redemption that honor the concrete particularities of the narrative's characters, circumstances, structure, and pattern of movement; and (2) explicit attention to the systematic interconnections among remarks made about redemption in this narrative and about other Christian beliefs.

Thus, for example, when I identified in chapter 1 five features typical of Christian talk of redemption that constrain any effort to explicate the theological meaning of the word *redemption*, I was attending to systematic relations between Christian beliefs about redemption and beliefs about other matters. So to note that redemption is understood as an "active relating" that makes a difference to the one related to is to note how its relations to beliefs about grace shape its explication. To note that redemption is understood as a complex relating of which both God and Jesus are the agent is to note how its relations to beliefs about incarnation shape its explication. To note redemption is understood as a way God actively relates to concrete human persons in concrete situations is to note how its relations to beliefs about human creatureliness shape its explication. To note that redemption is understood to be a difference God makes regarding both the evil human persons do and the evil they undergo is to note that it involves a distinction between beliefs about atonement and about eschatology. And to note that redemption is understood to take time is to note how its relations to beliefs about history and eschatology shape its explication. Not one of these systematic remarks provided any material answer to our question about the meanings of "redemption." But they did serve to remind us that whatever might be said about redemption must cohere with beliefs about grace, incarnation, human nature, atonement, eschatology, and history.

The structure of chapters 2 through 4 pushed systematic analysis further in regard to one of these related beliefs: incarnation. In those chapters I suggest that beliefs about the incarnation are answers to the question about Jesus' unsubstitutable personal identity—"Who is he?"—and are based on canonical Gospel narratives that render his identity. I noted that each of three strands in those narratives can be privileged as the one that defines Jesus' identity: narratives of his ministry of proclamation in word and healing; narratives of his passion and crucifixion; and narratives of his resurrection appearances. Drawing the distinction serves to remind us that each is an integral aspect of Jesus' identity, of what it means to speak of "incarnation," and that they are systematically interrelated and inseparable. In chapters 2 through 4 I suggest that each yields a different meaning to the claim that in Jesus God redeems the evil that human beings undergo. Thus the distinction among the three strands structures the three chapters. At the same time it serves to remind us that the three senses of redemption, while genuinely distinct, are systematically interrelated and inseparable.

In a different vein, when I distinguished in chapter 1 among three ways in which we use the phrase *to redeem* and related terms in ordinary English and suggested that Christians typically have extended each of them in metaphoric ways in talk about God's redeeming, I was drawing attention to systematic connections between theological and cultural modes of expression. To note that connection is to remind us that what we say about how the term *redemption* works in Christian talk (in English!) had better be coherent with what we are prepared to say about how the term works in ordinary English. More broadly, it reminds us that what we say about how language works in theological discourse in general had better be coherent with what we believe about how language works generally.

Theology that interweaves remarks about a narrative of evil undergone with attention to systematic interconnections between Christian beliefs about redemption and other Christian beliefs in this way
is systematically unsystematic. Remarks about the structure and
dynamics of the narrative of a particular situation of evil undergone
are unsystematic. Attention to the interconnections between remarks
made about redemption and other Christian beliefs is systematic.
Interweaving the two serves to remind us that the subject matter is
redemption, not the lives of the persons on which the narrative
focuses. In our case, it serves to remind us that the subject is some
meanings of redemption, not Sam and his family.

It should be clear, however, that while these theological reflections about redemption have been systematic, they do not begin to
amount to a systematic "doctrine of redemption." On the contrary,
they are no more than a fragment of a doctrine of redemption. Too
many topics have been omitted that would need to be included in a
proper doctrine of redemption—above all, the nature of redemption
from sin and from evil done as opposed to evil undergone, and its
consequences.

It should also be clear that this is not a plea for the view that theology should substitute "telling the story" for the systematic and rigorous analysis of Christian beliefs and the critique of arguments about
Christian beliefs. It does urge against the hegemony of one sort of
"theorizing" in theology on the grounds that it is inappropriate to
those Christian beliefs that are about "singularities." It also urges
that, in the sense meant here, "theorizing" is both appropriate and
necessary to other Christian beliefs.

REMEMBERING AND ANTICIPATING
REDEMPTION

The redemption of situations in which people have been overtaken by
horrendous evil is known only in retrospect. It is only as persons of faith
look back across a stretch of time that they recognize and acknowledge
God's redemptive relating to them in Jesus Christ in the midst of the
evil they undergo. This redemptive grace is recognized not in isolated
moments but only as its distinctive pattern is recognized in memory of

that time. It is truly acknowledged only as those who recognize God's redemptive relating live into it. But they can only live into it out of what they remember of their story of evil undergone.

The redemption of situations in which people have been overtaken by horrendous evil is always something still anticipated. God's redemptive grace is no more fully actualized in the momentary present than it has been in the remembered past. What is anticipated is an active relating by God in Jesus Christ that exhibits the same pattern as the gracious relating that is remembered. In one respect, to be sure, as God's "making up" for the world's bad performance by committing God's self in the person of Jesus to the promise of God's eschatological reign which re-creates the world, redemption is something God has already done once and for all. Once and for all it puts those for whom evil undergone makes the world an utterly unpromising context into a new and very promising context. Furthermore, in the resurrection of Jesus, God has already once and for all actually inaugurated the fulfillment of that promise. Nonetheless, redemption as "making good on a promise" is not yet fully actualized. In this respect it is something still anticipated. Moreover, God's "redemption from" the distorting power of evil suffered by God's solidarity with us in Jesus' passion has to be repeated anew on every occasion in which evil befalls individuals, distorting their identities. In this respect, as redemption from old situations is remembered, so redemption of new situations is anticipated.

Christianly speaking, then, so far as redemption is concerned, what is anticipated is what is remembered and what is remembered is what is anticipated. The redeemed live between memory and hope. Their life of liberation from distorted personal identities and release from vicious cycles of interaction is an endless living-into both what is remembered and what is hoped.

Is that anything more than a quite familiar set of psychological dynamics expressed in peculiarly Christian "symbols" like "grace," "incarnation," "Jesus' passion," "Jesus' resurrection"? Does not the insistence on "speaking Christianly," that is, "speaking from" the context of practices that make up the common life of Christian faith, communal and individual, simply mask, perhaps perversely, the fact that psychologizing is what is really going on?

I cheerfully acknowledge that there are striking formal parallels. Indeed, if such psychological dynamics are inherent in being human, and if there is a person with the identity described by the Synoptic Gospels' narratives (call him "Jesus"), and if there is a God who in and through that person (Jesus) relates to humankind overtaken by horrendous evil in a way that makes a redemptive difference to them as they are, with their psychological dynamics, then it is reasonable that God would work through just such psychological dynamics. Why would there not be formal parallels?

However, everything turns on the "ifs" about God and Jesus. *If* there is a person, Jesus, with the identity rendered by the narratives in the Synoptic Gospels, and *if* there is a God who relates redemptively to humankind in Jesus, *then* Christian remarks about redemption are not identical with nontheological psychological claims about the dynamics of human emotions. Such Christian remarks do not express the "same" ideas as the psychological analysis in an alternative "symbol system." Rather, the Christian remarks about redemption include claims that the psychological claims do not make. They include, for example, claims that God in Jesus is the agent of redemption. In the nature of the case no psychological analysis makes such a claim. The theological remarks also include the claim that the changes in persons' identities and lives that come with redemption are not finally self-generated nor evoked by interaction with other human beings; they are grace, freely given from beyond the entire network of human interactions. These and related claims are inherent in and inseparable from the practices that make up the common life of communities and persons of Christian faith. They may not necessarily be inconsistent with the claims psychological analyses make. They may, indeed, be false. For that matter, so may the psychological claims. What they clearly are, however, is different from each other, and the difference makes it impossible simply to collapse Christian talk of redemption into psychological analysis of the dynamics of deep changes in personal identities and in the patterns of interaction that make up persons' lives.

None of this amounts to a critique of psychological analysis or explanation. Nor does it amount to an argument for the truth of Christian remarks about redemption. My project is to try to answer Milton's question. My aim is to explicate some meanings of redemption, Christianly speaking, it is not to persuade anyone to speak Christianly about redemption or anything else. If one were to set out to do that, this would certainly not be the way to go about it!

IMAGINING REDEMPTION

Remembering redemption and anticipating redemption are imaginative acts differentiated by diverse temporal orientations. To *remember* redemption is to imagine it as a sequence of events in the past. To *anticipate* it is to imagine it as a sequence of events in the future. As I noted in chapter 3, putting the matter this way risks the objection that redemption, whether remembered or anticipated, is merely imaginary. I countered there that the verb *to imagine* does not necessarily mean to make up or invent. It may perfectly well mean "to grasp a complex concrete particular as some kind of whole," but that rejoinder requires a bit more explanation. The explanation can, in turn, do two further things. First, it can exhibit another strategy to keep this book focused on redemption and check any shift of focus to Sam and his family or to any other unique situation. Second, it can exhibit another strategy to keep clear the difference between a theological explication of redemption and formally similar psychological analyses of deep changes in the distortions of persons' identities and in the patterns of vicious cycles in their lives.

Because *to imagine, imagining,* and *imagination* are used in a variety of ways in ordinary English, their use can be confusing. The possibility of confusion comes clear when we note that we routinely credit people's imaginations both for ideas that we characterize as "imaginary," that is, fantastical, unreal, or false, and for ideas that we characterize as "imaginative," that is, insightful, advancing knowledge of the truth, or deepening understanding of reality. Really serious confusion arises when one type of use is unwarrantedly assumed to be the proper or standard use. In Western culture since the late sixteenth century *imagining* has been defined in *contrast* to *knowing*. The standard case of *knowledge* is defined as that which is produced by the physical sciences' disciplined, self-critical reasoning, rigorously constrained by controlled observation. The standard case of *imagination,* defined by contrast to such knowledge, is "fantasy," "the imaginary." By definition it is not knowledge, not true, "not real." Defined this way, "imagining" or "imagination" can be acknowledged to be the basis of creativity in the arts. It may be suspected to be the basis of religion, religious practices, and religious ideas, but imagining cannot be essential to acquiring knowledge.

There is no good reason to elevate this sense of "imagine" to the status of "standard" or normative sense. In other perfectly good senses of the term, "imagination" is as important to scientific inquiry as it is to the arts and to theology. As theologian H. Richard Niebuhr observed, the choice is never "between reason and imagination, but only between reasoning on the basis of adequate images and thinking with the aid of evil imaginations."[5]

There have been three levels of philosophical analyses of imagination.[6] The first has been part of philosophical inquiry into the conditions necessary for there to be any experience at all, or "transcendental" inquiry. This kind of inquiry investigates not a part or aspect of experience but the a priori structures of experience in general, in which imagination plays a role. Second, philosophers consider imagination when they inquire into the nature of perception. Third, philosophers consider imagination when they analyze the act of interpretation. I shall argue that the role of imagination in both perception and interpretation is inherent in Christian practices and Christian theological reflection.

No single philosophical proposal to clarify the concept of the imagination has commanded general acceptance. Nor has any proposed theory of "the imagination." What it is "to imagine" remains elusive. Perhaps it simply is not any one thing. This is not the place to review these efforts, and it is certainly not the place to attempt to succeed where they have failed. However, we can pick out one familiar sense of "to imagine," "imagining," "imagination," and the family of notions related to them that can be clarified as what I mean here in the phrase "imagining redemption."

In one sense "imagination" is a human ability; "to imagine" and "imagining" are the exercise of that ability. Imagination is the capacity to recognize the pattern in a complex whole that makes it the whole it is, and the capacity to use that pattern in several ways. Its exercise is inherent in acts of perception of complex wholes. The significance of this remark turns on an insight about the nature of complex wholes. As Garrett Green[7] has pointed out in *Imagining God*, his fine book on imagination in Christian theology, a "whole can be neither more nor less than the sum of its parts since it is not a *sum* at all. (If one is partial to mathematical analogies, it would be better to call the whole the *product* of its parts). . . . The logical, philosophical or grammatical point (its negative side, at least) has been put this way by one philosopher: 'Wholes are . . . quite incomparable with additive aggregations.'"[8]

Consequently a whole cannot be perceived simply by identifying some constituent part of it that makes it be the whole it is. Nor can a complex whole be recognized as what it is by perceiving its several parts and then mentally "adding them up" or putting them together. Rather, a complex whole is recognized by perceiving the pattern that makes it the whole it is.

A frequently used illustration of this point is the so-called "duck-rabbit" line drawing that may be recognized as either the outline of a duck's head or the outline of a rabbit's head. Because it is a simple line drawing, every *part* of the drawing is part of either the complex *whole* that is a picture of a duck's head or the complex *whole* that is a picture of a rabbit's head. It is not that some parts can be "added up" to construct a duck's head and some of the same parts plus other parts added up to construct a rabbit's head. All the parts of the line drawing make both pictures. What makes it a duck's head is a pattern recognized *as* a duck's head, which is different from another pattern recognized *as* a rabbit's head. In each case it is the pattern that makes the drawing be the complex *whole* drawing it is perceived as being. Green regularly calls the pattern that makes a particular whole what it is the whole's "constitutive pattern."

It is important to note that the ability to imagine a line drawing as a duck's head or as a rabbit's head is inseparable from having mastered the concepts "duck's head" and "rabbit's head." One is not born with the capacity to recognize a line drawing as either kind of head. One learns that ability. Nor does one learn it just by seeing a particular duck and a particular rabbit. One must learn to recognize line drawings as pictures of *types* of objects, such as ducks and rabbits, and to recognize some of them as pictures specifically of *heads* of those types of animals. Clearly, acquiring the ability to imagine a line drawing as a duck's head or rabbit's head involves mastering several concepts: concepts of picture, typical picture, duck, duck's head, rabbit, rabbit's head, and so forth. Imagining a line drawing *as* a duck's head or *as* a rabbit's head may not be the same thing as learning the concept of each, but it is inseparable from mastery of such concepts.

It is also important to note that perceiving a line drawing, for example, as a duck rather than as a rabbit and then perceiving it as a rabbit rather than a duck, is not in the ordinary sense of the term a matter of changing one's interpretation of the line drawing. The distinction between perceiving and interpreting becomes crucial here. When they are conflated with each other, then two different types of exercise of the capacities called "imagination" are confused with each other. The key difference can be brought out this way: interpreting is an intentional and deliberative activity. But the shifting figures is something we just see, without any deliberate act. Imagination is involved in interpreting as well as in perception, but in a different way. We shall return to this point in a moment.

While it is important to note that recognizing the pattern that makes a complex whole the whole it is involves images (i.e., it involves image-ing), the patterns are not necessarily picturable. As Green observes, the difference between a picture and an image "lies in the use or function: a picture reproduces; an image exemplifies."[9] What an image exemplifies is a constitutive pattern: "*Pattern*, though generally connoting visual experience, is more abstract than *image*, and less dependent on visual metaphor. . . . A pattern is an arrangement of elements in any medium."[10] Thus some patterns identified, say, in physics, although they cannot be pictured, can nonetheless be described mathematically. As Green points out, "Mathematics is a set of coherent patterns—a form of imagination."[11] So "[i]maginable is a broader term, including 'picturable,' but going beyond it to encompass other sorts of . . . [patterns] as well."[12]

"Imagination" is not only the human ability to recognize in an act of perception the constitutive pattern that makes a complex whole the whole it is; it is also the ability to use that pattern in various ways. The patterns may serve several functions in acts of imagining. For instance, it is an exercise of the imagination to use such a pattern to fill an exemplary function. That is, one may imagine the complicated pattern that constitutes an especially complex and (for that reason) obscure whole by using as its exemplar or ideal type a pattern that shows it forth in a relatively simple and straightforward manner. Such a pattern may thus function heuristically "by revealing the constitutive patterns in more complex aspects of our experience that might otherwise remain recalcitrant, incoherent, or bewildering."[13]

Such heuristic use of patterns in their exemplary function is extended in human beings' capacity to "recognize in accessible exemplars the constitutive organizing patterns of other, less accessible and more complex objects of cognition" including objects in "*both* the world of the imaginary *and* recalcitrant aspects of the real world."[14] Illustrations of heuristic use of exemplary patterns can as easily be identified in the work of natural scientists as in the work of poets or novelists. This is why "imagination" has both illusory and realistic senses.

Building on the work of philosopher of science Norwood Russell Hanson[15] and historian of science Thomas S. Kuhn,[16] Green has dubbed the sense of "imagination" with which we are working the "paradigmatic imagination." By a "paradigm" he means[17] a pattern that can function "as a normative exemplar of [the] constitutive structure"[18] of a complex whole. The "paradigmatic imagination," then, is "the ability of human beings to recognize in accessible exemplars the constitutive organizing patterns of other, less accessible and more complex objects of cognition. . . . Imagination is the means by which we are able to represent anything not directly accessible, including *both* the world of the imaginary *and* recalcitrant aspects of the real world; it is the medium of fiction as well as fact."[19]

. The paradigmatic imagination is at work in the cognitive act of interpretation. Earlier I noted that "imagining" should not be conflated with "interpreting." Nonetheless, interpreting certainly involves imagining. In interpreting a difficult text, H. Richard Niebuhr observed, in a frequently quoted remark, we sometimes find a "luminous sentence from which we can go forward and backward and so attain some understanding of the whole."[20] The paradigmatic imagination may employ the pattern of thought in the sentence heuristically to clarify the pattern of thought of the text as a complex whole. Sometimes in interpreting an especially complex novel the pattern of a particular episode or the pattern of a particular character's life can serve to clarify the pattern that makes a meaningful whole of the entire novel.

The exercise of imagination in the sense of "paradigmatic imagination" is inherent in the practices that make up the common life of communities of Christian faith and the individual lives of members of those communities, including practices of theological reflection. This is true simply because it is the exercise of abilities inherent in being human. Therefore, it is natural in the context of such practices to talk about *imagining* redemption of the awful concrete situations that befell the particular people comprising Sam's family. Indeed, Green's analysis suggests, imagining is inherent in those practices both at the level of interpretation and at the level of perception.

In the practices that make up Christian faith, both communal and individual, paradigmatic imagination is at work at one level in acts of interpretation. For example, the patterns of interaction between God's redemptive grace and human persons are both complex and obscure. So, in response to my friend Milton's question about the meaning(s) of "redemption" we relied on the heuristic function of the patterns of action in three types of accessible and relatively simple interactions to help interpret them: making up for poor performance; reclaiming something of one's own from control by another's power; and making good on a promise. These patterns function paradigmatically in our effort to interpret "redemption."

But then, wishing to give the elucidation of "redemption" greater concreteness, I sought to show some meanings of "redemption" for the particular sequence of appalling situations that Sam and his family underwent. At that juncture what is bewilderingly complex is the sequence of events that Sam's family undergoes; and what is inaccessible is the pattern of God's redemption in that sequence of events. So I relied on the heuristic function of each of three patterns of action in the Synoptic Gospels' narratives that render the unsubstitutable personal identity of Jesus of Nazareth: (1) Jesus' proclamation in word and healing as God promising the imminent inbreaking of God's end-time rule, a promising that makes up for the world's bad performance in the life of Sam's family by placing them in an entirely new and promising context; (2) Jesus' passion and crucifixion as God's solidarity with humankind in the horrendous evil it undergoes, freeing Sam's and his father's personal identities from their deeply distorting bondage to a horrendous past; and (3) Jesus' resurrection appearances as God's beginning to make good on God's promise of end-time re-creation of the world, including Sam and his family, breaking the vicious cycles that make their lives living deaths. Patterns of action and interaction in narratives that render the unsubstitutable personal identity of Jesus as the complex whole that it is serve our paradigmatic imaginations heuristically in our efforts to imagine what earthly redemptive difference Jesus can make here in these concrete situations. Patterns in the narrative-identity descriptions of Jesus thus function paradigmatically in our effort to interpret "redemption" concretely.

Such heuristic use of the Synoptic Gospels' narratives is itself warranted by an exercise of paradigmatic imagination in interpreting the normative, that is, canonical, texts with which communities of Christian faith live in all the practices that comprise their common life of faith. It is an act of interpretation of the Bible as a kind of canonical whole in which patterns in the narratives about Jesus function paradigmatically to clarify patterns that constitute the canon of normative texts (i.e., the Bible) as a meaningful whole. In addition, the liturgies Christians follow in practices of worship and the creeds they use in practices of worship and education of the faithful help warrant the way patterns of action in the Synoptic Gospels' narratives functioned heuristically to explain "redemptive" patterns of interaction in the lives of Sam and his family. Christians learn to *imagine* the world according to the paradigm exemplified by the creeds and by their liturgies.

This interlocking set of interpretive acts regarding the meanings of "redemption" involve "paradigmatically imagining" the terrible sequence of situations that Sam's family underwent in terms of the pattern of interactions that makes a complex whole of the personal identity of Jesus rendered by the Synoptic Gospels' narratives. Imagining redemption of that horrendous series of situations involves interpreting the story of that series in a certain way. It is a retrospective interpretation, memory's imagining redemption. The story of Sam and his family is difficult to interpret. What is dark and complex, obscured by inexplicable evil, threatens to make it mere meaningless chaos, no story at all, only a sad chronicle at best. However, their story includes the presence of the person of Jesus. The patterns that make a meaningful whole of Jesus' story—also a dark story threatened with meaninglessness by inexplicable evil—can thus function for the paradigmatic imagination as, in H. Richard Niebuhr's phrase, the "luminous sentence" from which "we can go forward and backward" in the story of Sam's family "and so attain some understanding of the whole" as a story of redemption begun though not fully actualized.

I noted in chapter 3 that imagining the story of what happened to Sam and his family as a story of the inauguration of God's redemption reverses narrative foreground and background. Initially, the foreground is the story of what befell Sam's family. The background is the story of what Jesus did and underwent. It is the story of one supporting figure, so to speak, in the foreground story. However, once the pattern that makes Jesus' story a meaningful whole functions heuristically in the effort to imagine redemption in the story of Sam's family, then that pattern places the story of Sam's family into a much larger narrative context. If the constitutive pattern of Jesus' story illumines Sam's family's story, it illumines the stories of all humankind. For the paradigmatic imagination, it serves heuristically to help grasp what makes a meaningful whole of every story that is otherwise inaccessible and unmanageably complex, darkened by evil and threatened with terminal meaninglessness. Every human story, including the story of the horrific events and situations Sam's family went through, is therefore incorporated into the constitutive pattern that drives the movement of the narrative that renders who Jesus is, making it the complex whole that it is. To imagine redemption of any concrete situation, such as that of Sam's family, is to include it within Jesus' story. That is critical to keeping our discussion focused on its subject: the meanings of God's redemptive relating to us in Jesus, not Sam and his family.

In addition to its role in interpretation, there is a second level at which paradigmatic imagination is at work in efforts to imagine redemption. Christians learn to *imagine the world* according to the paradigm exemplified by their creeds, by their liturgies, by their Scriptures interpreted as a canonical whole, and most decisively by the Synoptic Gospels' narrative rendering of Jesus' personal identity. Among other things, Christians learn to imagine the world according to that paradigm as a world redeemed. This is the level at which the paradigmatic imagination is inherent in perception rather than in interpretation.

Learning to imagine the world according to a paradigm exemplified in the ways previously noted is not limited to learning to interpret in certain ways what goes on in the world. It is also learning to perceive the world in certain ways. It is learning to perceive the world *as* gift; *as* radically dependent on God; as not just often productive of evil but *as* something ambiguous, at once good and profoundly distorted; *as* promised, an eschatological consummation by God; and *as* redeemed. Just as perceiving the same line drawing as a duck's head or as a rabbit's head is an exercise of the imagination rather than an intentional and deliberative act of interpretation, so are these ways that Christians learn to imagine the world acts of imagination and not acts of interpretation.

One might speak of these as learned ways of experiencing the world. Perceiving, after all, is a mode of conscious experience. However, if one did so speak it would be important to stress that "experience" here does not necessarily refer to any particular feelings. It is useful here to keep in mind a distinction that we can mark by assigning somewhat technical meanings to *feeling* and *emotion*. Let *feeling* name those self-conscious episodes that come and go fairly frequently and that vary in intensity. Think of phrases like "feeling a flash of rage," "feeling hurt," "feeling sorry for someone," "feeling a surge of elation," and so forth. Let *emotion* name relatively long-lasting states that are much more like attitudes. They need not be vivid to be authentic. They may not even be conscious most of the time. Think of how we speak of someone being "fundamentally happy," "abidingly grateful," "deeply hostile," and so on. Feelings may or may not attend perception of the world as gift, radically contingent, ambiguous, promised and promising, and redeemed. The feelings may vary enormously in clarity, intensity, and focus, or they may be entirely absent. What is inseparable from such perceptions of the world, however, is a set of appropriate emotions: gratitude and praise for gift; awe and maybe fear at radical contingency; grief, and perhaps remorse and repentance before ambiguity; joy at promise; gratitude, repentance, and joy at redemption.

What the perceptions and the related attitudes that Christians learn in accord with the paradigm exemplified in their creeds, liturgies, and Scriptures have in common are a set of concepts that they seek to master. We noted that the exercise of imagination in perceiving a line drawing as a duck's head or a rabbit's head required mastery of quite an array of concepts. So too, the exercise of paradigmatic imagination in perceiving the world as gift, or as redeemed, is inseparable from mastery of another array of concepts: grace, creation, love, sin, faith, end time, anticipation, hope, redemption.

When it is said that Sam and his family have only to live into the redemptive difference Jesus can make, "living into" is largely a matter of forming their capacities (1) for a certain paradigmatically imaginative interpretation of their own and other people's stories and (2) for perception or "experience" of their world. Insofar as imagining redemption is an act of imagination, it is something we can do for another and about another's life as well as about our own. We have attempted to imagine what redemptive difference Jesus can make for Sam and his family. That can be an invitation to them to do the same thing, both about themselves and about others' stories. Insofar as imagining redemption is an ingredient of one's own perception it is something we can only do for ourselves. That can only be an invitation to Sam's family to do it for themselves. The process of acquiring the capacities, including mastering the concepts, that are needed to perceive the world as created, be-graced, ambiguous, and redeemed is a major part of what is fostered by involvement in the practices that make up persons' lives of faith and the common life of communities of Christian faith. This is what the tradition has called "spiritual formation." There is no end to such "living into" God's redemptive relating to us. It has to be done afresh over and over. By the same token, there is no end to the imaginative task of explicating "redemption." It has to be done anew for each new situation of evil undergone or evil done as an exercise of the paradigmatic imagination.

> "People will faint from fear and foreboding of what is coming upon the world, for the powers of the heavens will be shaken. Then they will see 'the Son of Man coming in a cloud' with power and great glory. Now when these things begin to take place, stand up and raise your heads, because your redemption is drawing near."
>
> (Luke 21:26–28)[21]

Notes

Chapter 2: Promising Contexts

1. For example, Friedrich Schleiermacher, *The Christian Faith*, trans. H. R. Macintosh and J. S. Stewart (Edinburgh: T. & T. Clark, 1928), esp. 355–525; Wilhelm Herrmann, *The Communion of the Christian with God* (New York: Putnam's Sons, 1930).
2. For example, Adolf Harnack, *What is Christianity?* trans. Thomas Bailey Saunders (New York: Harper, 1957), esp. 1–78.
3. For example, Rudolf Bultmann, in *Existence and Faith: Shorter Writings of Rudolf Bultmann*, trans. Schubert Ogden (New York: Meridian, 1960), 58–93, "The Concept of Revelation in the New Testament," and 92–111, "The Historicity of Man and Faith."
4. For example, Paul Tillich, *Systematic Theology*, vol. 3 (Chicago: University of Chicago Press, 1963), passim.
5. Austin, *How to Do Things With Words* (Oxford: Oxford University Press, 1965). For what follows see especially Lectures 1, 2, and 12.

Chapter 3: Fellow Sufferer

1. Frei, *The Identity of Jesus Christ* (Philadelphia: Fortress Press, 1975).
2. Brown, *The Gospel According to John* (New York: Doubleday, 1966), 369.
3. Lewis, *The Problem of Pain* (London: Geoffrey Bles, 1940).
4. Brunner, *Der Mensch im Widerspruch* (Berlin: Furche-Verlag, 1937). The English translation by Olive Wyon (Philadelphia: Westminster Press, 1947) is titled *Man in Revolt*.
5. Murdoch, *The Unicorn* (New York: Viking, 1963), 188–89.
6. Allen, *The Path of Perfect Love* (Boston: Cowley Press, 1992), 38.

Chapter 4: Breaking Vicious Cycles

1. Kierkegaard, *Works of Love* (New York: Harper, 1962).
2. See Bultmann, *Theology of the New Testament*, trans. Kendrick Grobel (New York: Scribner's Sons, 1954), 1:306–14 and 2:95–100.
3. Volf, *Exclusion and Embrace* (Nashville: Abingdon Press, 1996), 92.
4. Williams, *Resurrection* (New York: Pilgrim Press, 1984), 24.
5. Schleiermacher, *The Christian Faith*, trans. H. R. Macintosh and J. S. Stewart (Edinburgh: T. & T. Clark, 1928), 12–18.

Coda

1. See William Clebsch and Charles R. Jaekle, *Pastoral Care in Historical Perspective* (Englewood Cliffs, NJ: Prentice Hall, 1964).
2. For recent helpful explorations of the theological substance and criteria of many such practices see Dorothy Bass, ed., *Practicing our Faith* (San Francisco: Jossey-Bass, 1997), and Miroslav Volf and Dorothy Bass, eds., *Practicing Theology* (Grand Rapids: Wm. B. Eerdmans Publishing Co., 2002).
3. For a somewhat more fully developed version of these views see David H. Kelsey, *To Understand God Truly* (Louisville, KY: Westminster/John Knox Press, 1992).
4. Gunton, *The Actuality of Atonement* (Grand Rapids: Wm. B. Eerdmans Publishing Co., 1989).
5. Niebuhr, *The Meaning of Revelation* (New York: Macmillan, 1941), 108.
6. I am indebted to Garrett Green for this typology: *Imagining God* (Grand Rapids: Wm. B. Eerdmans Publishing Co., 1998), 65–66.
7. Ibid., 75, 84.
8. Ibid., 51, quoting Andras Angyal, "The Structure of Wholes," *Philosophy of Science* 6 (1939): 25–37.
9. Green, *Imagining God*, 93–94.
10. Ibid., 94.
11. Ibid., 76.
12. Ibid., 77.
13. Ibid., 53.
14. Ibid., 66; emphasis in original.
15. Hanson, *Patterns of Discovery: An Enquiry into the Conceptual Foundations of Science* (Cambridge: Cambridge University Press, 1958).
16. Kuhn, *The Structure of Scientific Revolutions*, 2nd ed., enl. (Chicago: University of Chicago Press, 1970).
17. See Green, *Imagining God*, 49–54.
18. Ibid., 67.
19. Ibid., 66.
20. Niebuhr, *The Meaning of Revelation*, 93.
21. From the Gospel appointed by the Common Lectionary for the First Sunday of Advent, Year C.